DAYSPRING

ANNE S. WHITE

Victorious Ministry Through Christ, Inc.
P.O. Box 1804, Winter Park, Florida 32790

First Edition 1971 Logos International
Second Edition 1990 Victorious Ministry Through Christ, Inc.

ISBN - 0-9605178-2-0
Library of Congress Catalog Card Number 90-090277
Printed in the United States of America

DAYSPRING

Author of

Healing Adventure
Healing Devotions
Trial by Fire
Study Adventure in Trial by Fire
Jesus, All in All
Freed to Live
The Transforming Power of God

Dedicated to the glory of God
and to those who prayerfully listen in love
to the Word of God and in obedience to His Son
are led by the Holy Spirit in lives that glorify Him

PREFACE

THE MASTER SPEAKS to His disciples today through the Word
of God and through the inspiration of His Holy Spirit. He
illumines our minds and encourages us through prophecies,
through the word of Wisdom and the word of Knowledge.
Some of these writings were given by Him to this listener early
one morning as she entered into a particularly difficult chapter
of life. They have been tested and found helpful in the labora-
tory of her life. They are shared with the prayer that others too
may find strength for the day as they pause each morning to
meditate on the selected Scriptures and to listen for the Voice
of the Master through these prophecies. He teaches, He com-
forts, He strengthens, He guides, He exhorts His disciples
today—"forth-telling His Good News."

Although any translation may be used, the author has
found the Revised Standard Version of the Bible to be most
meaningful.

The author gratefully acknowledges help given by several
friends who prayerfully assisted in typing and/or editing this
manuscript. Much gratitude is due my patiently loving husband
and my English prayer partners, Jeanne and Michael Harper,
without whose help this manuscript would not be published.

FOREWORD

OUR AGE has largely lost the art of listening. Never before has the world talked so loudly or so volubly, to such little effect. The Church is no better. Some even doubt whether God still speaks today.

It is with this background in mind that I am glad to commend Mrs. Anne White's book DAYSPRING. My wife and I have known the author since 1963, and have personally benefited from her ministry in many ways. Her personal friendship and encouragement has meant a lot to us. We know that she is one of the few who have learned to listen as well as speak to God, and this has proved of great importance in her gifted healing ministry. She has also learned how to listen to people.

One knows the author well enough to say that she is not in this book placing the gift of prophecy on an equal footing with the scriptures. Prophecy should always be judged by scripture. But God *does* speak today through prophecies—as He did in the days of the apostles—always confirming, never contradicting, the scriptures. I hope that many will use these readings and prophecies—one for each day of the year—in addition to their regular devotional habits; and that they will not limit the Holy Spirit, but expect Him to speak to them in ways additional to these written prophecies. Above all else I trust this book will teach us all to be better *listeners*. I believe it will.

The Rev. Michael Harper
Fountain Trust
London, England

SUNDAY St. John 14:26-27

Peace I leave with you; my peace I give to you; not as the world gives do I give to you. Let not your hearts be troubled, neither let them be afraid. St. John 14:27

Be still and know that I am your Lord speaking to you. Take hold of My Peace within you and let me draw you into the safe haven of My indwelling Peace. The storms of life cannot overcome you if you remain centered in Me. Look to Me, not the gales about you. Satan would deceive you to think that what you face is impossible. He would tell you that the course of following Me is too turbulent. But in My Will is your Peace. Look to Me. Leave the details to Me to unfold for you as My Love grows in you. Abide in Me.

MONDAY I Corinthians 6:19-20

Do you not know that your body is a temple of the Holy Spirit within you, which you have from God? You are not your own. I Corinthians 6:19

My child, do not be afraid to let Me bring forth in you My creativity of spirit, for I need temples in which My Spirit can dwell. I have purposes for you beyond your human understanding. They can be fulfilled only by My Wisdom and Love indwelling you in a permanent relationship that begins now and continues into all eternity. Yield yourself to Me so that My Will can be done in you today—My highest Will, not just My permissive Will!

TUESDAY   St. John 15:5-8

Bv this my Father is glorified, that you bear much fruit, and so prove to be my disciples.   St. John 15:8

You are entering into a new phase of ministry in which there will be more of Me and less of you. The things you need will be drawn to you effortlessly, and My work will be done through you without strain. Abide in Me—and let My creativity flow through you to meet the needs of others whom I will send to you. You need have no fear: the sap will flow through the branch to bear much better fruit as you become more vine-conscious.

WEDNESDAY   Proverbs 3:5-6

In all your ways acknowledge him, and he will make straight your paths.   Proverbs 3:6

You have given much of yourself to Me but you have not given all. You are still holding back one area of your life for yourself. You trust Me in all the other areas, but in this one you are not willing to accept My Will. My ways are higher than your ways. My Grace is sufficient for you. Release this area to Me. Trust in Me to make your paths straight: to make you more effective in My service today.

THURSDAY   II Corinthians 12:7-10

My grace is sufficient for you, for my power is made perfect in weakness.   II Corinthians 12:9 (in part)

When the pressures of the day seem too great, look quickly to Me. This upward look opens the door in your being for My Strength, My Wisdom to flow into you and through you into the situations around you. My Grace, My spiritual Power, My Love are sufficient for you! Rest for a moment in Me—then return to your duties with My inner Peace in control. When you are the weakest, I can be strongest in you if you surrender to Me full control of each problem.

FRIDAY   Galatians 5:15-18

But I say, walk by the Spirit.   Galatians 5:16a

The moments you spend with Me are not wasted. I can compensate for them in your time schedule. You think you are too busy to pause for the upward look. That is Satan's voice, not Mine. I call you to walk with Me through each day: walk by the Spirit! Let Me plan your time schedule and let Me stretch minutes as you give the day to Me. Let it be *My* day *in you.* I can open closed doors more easily than you can imagine possible.

SATURDAY   I Corinthians 12:12-13,27

Now you are the body of Christ and individually members of it.   I Corinthians 12:27

I need a Body—My Church is that Body. You—each of you—are a part of My Body. My Love will bring healing to the Body and through the Body to the world about you if you are willing to let Me use you as I choose. Each member is important. There is no age limit: only willingness to be used by Me *whenever, wherever* I call you.

SUNDAY   Psalm 19:1,14

The heavens are telling the glory of God; and the firmament proclaims his handiwork.   Psalm 19:1

Rejoice in beauty that is around you! See the wonder of each flower that grows from a tiny bud and unfolds into full bloom; the beauty of a sunset sky that is streaked with ever-changing colors; the smooth, glassy blue of the lake that awhile ago was ruffled as a boat sped by. Learn from the bud patience that awaits the unfolding of My Plan of perfection. Learn from the sky that life is changeable but I can harmonize all the colors and bring beauty out of them—even storm clouds. Learn from the lake to be still. After the thrusts of life, regain composure in Me.

MONDAY   St. Luke 23:44-49

Now when the centurion saw what had taken place, he praised God, and said, "Certainly this man was innocent!" St. Luke 23:47

Stand on the promises in My Holy Word. Feed your mind and spirit each day as you meditate on a passage of Scripture. You can become in your meditation one of the crowd that listened to My words in Galilee. You can be the one who received My healing touch. You can be the centurion at the foot of My Cross. Live with Me through My earthly

Life and let My Life speak to your heart. Hear My words spoken to you in the midst of your life. Let My resurrection Life bear fruit in your life today.

TUESDAY   St. Matthew 5:44-48

You, therefore, must be perfect, as your heavenly Father is perfect.   St. Matthew 5:48

Unless you remain in union with Me, you cannot keep this commandment. You have been broken; your pride has been humbled so that there may be less of self and more of Me. No one else can hurt you (not even your enemies). But your own reactions to them can rob you of your inner peace and composure, your inner joy of My abiding Presence. When you cannot love someone in your own nature, let My Nature be formed in you: let Me love him *through* you.

WEDNESDAY   I Peter 5:8-11   Right! Jan 14, 98

And after you have suffered a little while, the God of all grace, who has called you to his eternal glory in Christ, will himself restore, establish, and strengthen you.   I Peter 5:10

Satan is the great deceiver. When he cannot claim your heart by luring you into his temptations, he will try to poison your mind with his doubts. He would try to make you believe that you are too weak or too tired—and especially that you are too busy. Stand firm on My Promises. In your weakness My Strength will be perfected. In your weariness of spirit and mind and body, rest in Me and be refilled and renewed and refreshed. Let Me take dominion.

THURSDAY   Psalm 118:24,28-29

This is the day which the Lord has made; let us rejoice and be glad in it.   Psalm 118:24

This closeness you feel with Me in the early morning hours is your re-fueling for the day. It is in this time of resting in My Peace that your spiritual batteries will be re-charged and your strength renewed. Do not keep Me waiting. Give Me joyously the first fruits of the day and center in Me. Then return to this centering from time to time throughout the day as each need arises. I will be within you and My Love will manifest itself through you. Rejoice in Me. Praise Me in the Spirit. Live in thanks-giving!

FRIDAY   St. John 7:37-39

On the last day of the feast, the great day, Jesus stood up and proclaimed, "If any one thirst, let him come to me and drink."   St. John 7:37

My strength will be sufficient for this day and My Joy will replenish your need to be filled—over and over again. Come to Me and drink. The rivers of living water welling up within you will renew your spirit as they flow through you to meet the needs of My other children. Give Me away to all who are seeking to hear the deeper call of My Voice. The well will not run dry, for My Spirit is inexhaustible.

SATURDAY   St. John 14:20-21

He who has my commandments and keeps them, he it is who loves me; and he who loves me will be loved by my Father, and I will love him and manifest myself to him. St. John 14:21

Obedience is My condition for usefulness. If you love Me, you will prove it by receiving My commands and obeying them. The world looks to intellect or temporal power as necessary to greatness, but My Father and I reveal ourselves to the one who in humility and love is obedient to My Will. No matter how weak you may feel, you are usable when you are willing to be used by Me in *My way*, *My place* and *My time*.

SUNDAY   Isaiah 26:3-4

Thou dost keep him in perfect peace, whose mind is stayed on thee, because he trusts in thee.   Isaiah 26:3

The world wants security. It cries out for peace—and there is no peace! But you know the secret, for you are My disciple. If your mind is stayed on Me, I will keep you in perfect Peace. My Peace does not depend on circumstances. You can be calm in the midst of a storm as you *fix your gaze on Me*—not on the problems. Let Me be the mainstay in the ship of life—your daily life.

MONDAY St. Matthew 11:28-30

Take my yoke upon you, and learn from me; for I am gentle and lowly in heart, and you will find rest for your souls. St. Matthew 11:29

Come unto Me and I will refresh you. When you are weary, heavy laden with anxiety, troubled in your heart, you do not need to depend on a cigarette or a drink to lift your spirits. You can look to Me and lift the loads to Me. *Release them into My hands* in the prayer of surrender and pray in the Spirit. Return to your work refreshed by My Spirit. When you are yoked to Me, your burdens will become lighter. Learn from Me the secret of surrender.

TUESDAY Hebrews 4:14-16

Let us then with confidence draw near to the throne of grace, that we may receive mercy and find grace to help in time of need. Hebrews 4:16

When you are weak, remember that I am your High Priest interceding for you. Satan's nagging voice will make you condemn yourself and lose heart. In My Love, there is not condemnation but forgiveness of sin. My Holy Spirit convicts you to *repent* and accept My Power to overcome sin in your life—to receive mercy and help in each need. Hold fast to your confession of faith in Me and let My forgiveness bring Joy.

WEDNESDAY   St. Matthew 7:1-3

Why do you see the speck that is in your brother's eye, but do not notice the log that is in your own eye? St. Matthew 7:3

Satan can poison your mind through criticism. You have been judging. Judge not, else you yourself are judged. The boomerang of criticism will return to the one who flings it out to another. Your discernment of spirits is a gift of My Holy Spirit. It is given to you—not to enable you to criticize but to pray. Pray for the one in whom you see this lack— that she may be filled by My Holy Love and Wisdom. Pray for yourself: beware when you think you stand—lest you fall!

THURSDAY   II Timothy 1:6-7

For God did not give us a spirit of timidity but a spirit of power and love and self-control. II Timothy 1:7

Fear robs you, My child, of your inner peace and composure. Fear is of Satan when it paralyzes you or distorts your true vision. The gift of discernment is given you *not to make you fear*—but to pray. You have received the gift of the Holy Spirit that you may minister to the needs about you with courage and in the Power of My Name. My perfect Love casts out fear. You can take authority over Satan's attacks and keep a sound mind. During his attacks, claim My Victory!

FRIDAY Ephesians 6:10-18

Put on the whole armor of God, that you may be able to stand against the wiles of the devil. Ephesians 6:11

The times are troubled and My "prayer warriors" must become strong enough in My Love to discern evil and not be fearful. Fear cripples the work I would do through you. My troops must be disciplined and not retreat each time Satan threatens or assaults. Put on the whole armor of God: the helmet of knowledge of My saving Grace; the breastplate of My Righteousness in you (not your own); the girdle of My Truth, My Way, My Life; the shoes of the Good News of My Peace; the shield of faith like a great tent about you; the sword of the Spirit, My Living Word spoken through you. Having done all, STAND.

SATURDAY I John 1:6-10

If we confess our sins, he is faithful and just, and will forgive our sins and cleanse us from all unrighteousness. I John 1:9

When you feel this heaviness of spirit, open yourself wider to Me through confession of your sins. Open all the little windows of relationships and let the warmth of My Love shine through them. In the house of life there is need for cleansing. Open the closets. Air the musty relationships in the antiseptic rays of My Light. Housecleaning can be a joyous experience in your life. Let My spiritual vacuum cleaner suck out of you the grit of edgy relationships, the silt of self, the dirt of gossip. Cleanse your heart in the purifying stream of My Blood shed for you personally.

SUNDAY   St. John 6:48-58

He who eats my flesh and drinks my blood abides in me, and I in him.   St. John 6:56

My Love is filling you—every cell, every nerve, every tissue, every fibre of your being. My Love is sufficient for *all* the needs of those about you. My Body is transfusing your body as you receive Me at Holy Communion. You are receiving this spiritual transfusion—cell after cell is being renewed. My Spirit is being poured into you infilling your whole being, healing the whole person—so that you may be a cleaner channel of My healing Power to others. Claim My Power, My Presence in each one for whom you pray today.

MONDAY   St. Matthew 6:25-34

But seek first his kingdom and his righteousness, and all these things shall be yours as well.   St. Matthew 6:33

My child, you are fearful again because you have taken your eyes off Me. You have become anxious. You have been trying to solve all your problems by yourself—on your own timetable. You are *manipulating people and circumstances—* instead of surrendering them to Me. You need only repent and accept *at once* My divine forgiveness. My Peace does not come to your heart through rationalizing! But, through repentance, you can receive the healing forgiveness of My Love.

TUESDAY   Galatians 5:1; Ephesians 2:8-10

For freedom Christ has set us free; stand fast therefore, and do not submit again to a yoke of slavery.   Galatians 5:1

Are you still punishing yourself, my child? Are you not willing to *accept* what *I did for you on the Cross* when I took your sins upon Myself and bore the full brunt of them and rose to break the power of sin? In My Resurrection your sins were canceled—but this will be effective in your life only *if you claim My forgiveness*. Accept it. And go forth in My Joy to proclaim My forgiveness to others.

WEDNESDAY   St. John 12:46-48; St. Matthew 7:1-5

I have come as light into the world, that whoever believes in me may not remain in darkness.   St. John 12:46

Too many have taken it upon themselves to proclaim My judgment. I came not to judge the world but to save the world. I came to set the captives free; to open the prison doors of the past through the cleansing, healing stream of My Light—shining in the darkness. And the darkness of the world has never been able to overcome it. Judge not, pray much. *Be* My channel for Light to flow into the darkness. *Be* a candle set on fire with My Love to light the Way to those in darkness.

THURSDAY   Galatians 6:1-7

Bear one another's burdens, and so fulfil the law of Christ. Galatians 6:2

I need an army—an army of "stretcher-bearers." Will you enlist today—to carry the wounded from the battlefield of life into My temples of healing? You can bring them to Me at any one of My altars—in any Church. You can bring them to Me at the altar in your "secret closet." You can make an altar for Me to be present in your heart—beside every sickbed in a hospital, at the scene of an accident, in a crisis. Will you give Me room in your heart for an altar? Not just for today—but *every* day?

FRIDAY   St. John 13:12-17

If I then, your Lord and Teacher, have washed your feet, you also ought to wash one another's feet.   St. John 13:14

I need an army—an army of "foot-washers." Are you willing to wash My feet? Then wash the feet of My other children who are traveling the hot dusty roads of life. Wash their feet with the same tenderness you would show Me. Do it as if to Me!

SATURDAY I Corinthians 10:12-13

No temptation has overtaken you that is not common to man. God is faithful, and he will not let you be tempted beyond your strength, but with the temptation will also provide the way of escape, that you may be able to endure it. I Corinthians 10:13

Satan is trying to distract you from My true purpose for your life. The devil knows the best way to attack you—your weakest spot. He can use uncommitted people to wear down your resistance to his wiles. The Father never tempts His children but He allows Satan to exist during this present time. My strength is always available to you: in every temptation I can make a way out, even where to your eyes there is *no* way! I can use the devil's temptation to test your faith, your surrender. I will *bring* you through to greater Victory—if you *claim* the Power of My Blood over the situation.

SUNDAY St. John 14:6-7; St. Matthew 7:15-20; I John 4:1-3

Thus you will know them by their fruits. St. Matthew 7:20

The Father is not the author of confusion but of Peace. Satan loves to confuse you. He tries to persuade you to take your eyes off *THE Truth* by deceiving you with his *half-truths!* The false prophets often take a half-truth and attempt to make it the whole. *Test* the spirits, for many false prophets have gone into the world. The ravening wolves would devour the lambs. I am *The Truth, The Way* and *The Life.* Study My words in Scripture and check your guidance against them. Let My Holy Spirit lead you into My Truth.

MONDAY   St. Luke 16:19-31; Hebrews 9:27-28

He said to him, "If they do not hear Moses and the prophets, neither will they be convinced if some one should rise from the dead."   St. Luke 16:31

Those who cling to the heresies of "reincarnation" and "universal salvation" do not listen to My warnings. They try to substitute their own ideas of justice and refuse to accept the Truth of My Word. Each life is judged (after death) by the merciful Heavenly Father on the basis of His understanding of the person's sin. Those who do not put their trust in Me during this life on earth cancel out what I made available for them on the Cross. Those who have chosen to deny Me in this life on earth make My death of no value to themselves. They would detest an eternity of My Presence! The Father in His Mercy and Justice allows each person to choose in this lifetime, but there is *no* coming back after death for a second chance. If there were, there would have been no need for My atoning death. Such heresies deny salvation by grace for they emphasize salvation by works.

TUESDAY   St. Matthew 26:36-45; I Peter 2:24-25

He himself bore our sins on his body on the tree, that we might die to sin and live to righteousness. By his wounds you have been healed.   I Peter 2:24

Come to *Me* when you are fearful or in doubt—even as I came to the Father (not to others) in the Garden of Gethsemane. Speak to Me *honestly* of your doubts and fears. Then claim the Power of My Blood over your thoughts and emotions and symptoms. I died for *you*, My child. Accept My Victory for you *now!* By My stripes you are healed. I am your Guardian.

WEDNESDAY Hebrews 13:8; St. John 8:12; St. Matthew 6:24

Jesus Christ is the same yesterday and today and for ever. Hebrews 13:8

Something is being pulled out of you in this deep cleansing —a splinter from the past that has been festering within you, a secret root to your troubles. Give this painful memory—the one you have never shared with anyone else—to Me. Let Me shine My healing antiseptic Light into this dark corner of your life. Let Me enter into the "room of relationship" that you have for years held barred and locked up within you. Let Me open wide the windows and air out the mustiness of buried bitterness, jealousy, and fear. Let Me cleanse the old tape recording with My healing, purifying Love.

THURSDAY St. John 17:1-2,14-21

I do not pray for these only, but also for those who believe in me through their word. St. John 17:20

My power is greater than all powers on earth, but you must claim this afresh each day. Look to Me again and again throughout the day. Claim the Power of My Blood over your home, your loved ones as you give them to Me today. Claim My protection over your car and your work: give them each day to Me. Satan will often try to attack you through these persons and concerns if they are not committed to Me. My protection is sufficient for all your loved ones and for all that deeply concerns you.

FRIDAY   Ephesians 1:16-23

I do not cease to give thanks for you, remembering you in my prayers.   Ephesians 1:16

My beloved child, go forth with your head held high, a smile on your lips and a song in your heart, for I go before you to prepare the way for this new ministry. I am with you and within you. You have nothing to fear. My Love surrounds you like a great shield, protecting you from all evils, doubts, uncertainties, and fears. Keep your eyes on Me. I lead the way—today.

SATURDAY   Galatians 5:22-25

If we live by the Spirit, let us also walk by the Spirit. Galatians 5:25

Your thinking processes are now being directed by My Holy Spirit to calm, clear, positive, creative thinking. It has been a necessary part of your new ministry that you have been acquainted with evil so that you might learn how to deal with it. You need a prayer partner in this new ministry. Let Me choose the right one. Your work will be difficult at first but with great fruit-bearing after a time. Be patient. Be persevering. Let Me bring forth the results through you. Let Me love through you those who have deep needs. Keep surrendered to

Me—*not to them!* Be free of them; for this flow of My healing Love must have a clear channel to reach them.

SUNDAY   Romans 8:9-11

If the Spirit of him who raised Jesus from the dead dwells in you, he who raised Christ Jesus from the dead will give life to your mortal bodies also through his Spirit which dwells in you.   Romans 8:11

Your body is being filled with My Love, giving new vitality in all things, new harmony. Your heart is being filled with new Courage, new Love—radiating through your whole being to draw others to Me. My child, you are to reveal Me to others in ways beyond your present understanding. Trust Me to release My Power in and through you when I bring to you those in need of this ministry of My healing Love.

MONDAY   I Corinthians 10:9-13

No temptation has overtaken you that is not common to man. God is faithful, and he will not let you be tempted beyond your strength, but with temptation will also provide the way of escape, that you may be able to endure it. I Corinthians 10:13

Too much emphasis on Satan's activities can distract you from Me. Some of your problems have not been assaults by the enemy but I have tested you to see if you have learned the lesson of full dependence on Me. There is a time in the growth of each soul when "dryness" is necessary to force deeper root growth. Pray always to know—to discern—which it is in each case. The plant growing in rocky ground must send its roots down deeper than the one springing out of lush soil. Seek Me on the deepest levels of your consciousness. Be still and let My Peace invade these deeper subconscious levels of your being.

TUESDAY   Psalm 46:10

Be still, and know that I am God. I am exalted among the nations, I am exalted in the earth!   Psalm 46:10

Be still this moment—in your body, your mind, your spirit. Relax each tense muscle from head to toe. Tense and relax again. Hold the word "Peace" in your mind; and as it fades into memory, let a new thought of the word "Peace" drop again into your deep subconscious mind. Hold it in stillness—in quietness—in confident trust that My will for you is Peace. "Be still and know that I am God"—and take hold of My Peace within you. Take hold of My Love within you—My Power to guide and strengthen and sustain you. In quiet, confident trust you will find My strength for this day.

WEDNESDAY   St. Matthew 11:28

Come to me, all who labor and are heavy laden, and I will give you rest.   St. Matthew 11:28

Rest in Me this morning and *know* that I will not fail you. The might of My righteousness is with you to defend you throughout this day. My Love will comfort you; My Wisdom will guide you. Rest in Me in spirit as you go through this day. When you feel pulled apart by many distractions, stop your work and *rest in Me* again for a few minutes. Let your mind create a picture of still waters and lush pastures. Know Me as the Shepherd who leads His sheep in safety beside these waters and into areas of Peace. Then return to your work with new vigor. I can compensate for the minutes spent in My Presence.

THURSDAY Galatians 5:22-25

And those who belong to Christ Jesus have crucified the flesh with its passions and desires. Galatians 5:24

The Power of My Holy Spirit is available to transform you: to bring forth in your life the fruit of Love, Joy, Peace, and Patience. I give you opportunities to grow these fruits in your life. As you claim Me in each relationship, My Love can love the unlovable through you. My Joy can transcend circumstances so that you will be joyous even in times of sadness. My Peace can *keep you centered in Me*—even in times of testing. Let My true humility replace your false humility today.

FRIDAY Acts 10:38

How God anointed Jesus of Nazareth with the Holy Spirit and with power; how he went about doing good and healing all that were oppressed by the devil, for God was with him. Acts 10:38

My goodness is different from the world's "do-goodism." Let My indwelling Spirit bring forth the fruit of goodness in your life—not just "good works" for themselves alone. Let Me use your life—as I incarnate Myself in You—to express My healing Love, an antidote to the devil's oppressions. The anointing of My Holy Spirit can bring forth goodness in your life that you cannot manufacture of your own human resources. Let others, seeing this goodness, be drawn to commit their lives to Me. Let Me begin a little "chain reaction" of goodness through your life today.

SATURDAY   St. Matthew 27:11-26

So when Pilate saw that he was gaining nothing, but rather that a riot was beginning, he took water and washed his hands before the crowd, saying, "I am innocent of this man's blood; see to it yourselves."   St. Matthew 27:24

You cannot wash your hands of the responsibility of living in today's world. You cannot walk away from its problems as Pilate tried to do, washing his hands of the guilt of My Bloodshed. You are called as a member of My Body the Church to share Me. In the stream of reality today, you cannot run and hide as Peter tried to do. You are called to deeper prayer commitment—and whatever action of My Love proceeds from that, even if it means a Cross in your life. There is no "escape from reality" for My followers. You are to go *through* the Cross to find the glory side in My Joy!

SUNDAY   I Corinthians 1:18-31; St. Luke 2:46-47

For the word of the cross is folly to those who are perishing, but to us who are being saved it is the power of God.
I Corinthians 1:18

My Cross is still a stumbling block to the learned today who are perishing—drowning in their own intellectual seas of doubt. My Father made the wisdom of the world as foolishness when He spoke through Me as a child of twelve in the temple in Jerusalem. The Power of My Blood is not given to the intellectual debaters but rather to those who in humility will accept My Cross in their lives. My life-giving Power transforms the life of the sinner who repents and turns to Me for resurrection. My Father has chosen to use the redeeming of the weak to shame those who trust in their own human wisdom and righteousness. Will you accept His redemption and put your intellect under the Power of My Blood today?

MONDAY   St. John 21:15-17

When they had finished breakfast, Jesus said to Simon Peter, "Simon, son of John, do you love me more than these?" He said to him, "Yes, Lord; you know that I love you." He said to him, "Feed my lambs."   St. John 21:15

There are people in this sad cold world who pay a fee to have someone telephone to tell them that they are loved. Where are My followers? Did I not tell you (like Peter) to feed My lambs and sheep? People are *hungering* for Love. In their spiritual blindness, they seek artificial expressions of human love instead of the all-encompassing Love I am yearning to give them! Will you be one today who will accept the ministry of giving My divine compassion to others? Will you be a "giver" instead of a "getter?" For it is in giving out to others that you will receive My greatest blessings. It is in loving others that you will find My wellsprings of divine Love replenishing your own supply.

TUESDAY   St. John 15:13

Greater love has no man than this, that a man lay down his life for his friends.   St. John 15:13

My earthly life was laid down voluntarily for you because your sins had to be atoned. Someone had to pay the price that you might go free and become once more at one with God. When you confess your sins and accept Me as Savior and Lord of your life, the burden of guilt is lifted by My forgiveness. My Love floods your whole being: body, mind, spirit, and soul. There is healing Power in this experience for those whom no medicine or operations have been able to heal of their burdens of guilt. There is no greater love than My Love, for I have *taken* your burden of guilt from you.

WEDNESDAY   St. John 15:12; Romans 5:8

This is my commandment, that you love one another as I have loved you.   St. John 15:12

As My Love is used to heal you, let it flow through you for the healing of others. This will complete your own healing. If there is someone you cannot humanly love, *let Me love* this person *through you*. Ask Me to channel My Love into this relationship for the healing of *both* of you. I have loved you while you were yet a sinner. Love him with My Love. Love him as I have loved you.

THURSDAY   St. Mark 3:32-35

Whoever does the will of God is my brother, and sister, and mother.   St. Mark 3:35

My family are those who *do* the Will of God. It was hard for My earthly family to accept this, and at first it will be hard for your blood relations too. They cannot see that there is a "divine blood-relationship" in your life now. Love them in tangible ways that they can accept. Remember to do the little kind, loving things for your family—as if you were doing them to Me. Let them *see* that they do not have to be *jealous* of the new family-in-Christ relationships. Ask Me often: "Am I to minister to those within my home now or to those of the new family?" Be *obedient.*

FRIDAY   St. John 15:16

You did not choose me, but I chose you and appointed you that you should go and bear fruit and that your fruit should abide; so that whatever you ask the Father in my name, he may give it to you.   St. John 15:16

I have called you into a ministry of fruit-bearing and you have accepted this appointment. In My Name *go*, knowing that what you ask in My Nature of Love will be given you. Asking in My Name means asking those things that are within My Nature. I have commanded you to love, so *be guided by My Love.* Ask in faith. Standing on My Words (for they will help you), now hold fast against doubts and fears. Ask much—but always in My Nature of Love.

SATURDAY   St. Matthew 3:8-9,11-12

Bear fruit that befits repentance.   St. Matthew 3:8

My Spirit is upon you for I have anointed you for this new ministry. My baptism is with the Holy Spirit and with purifying fire. The chaff will be burned, but the wheat will be gathered in to feed many. You have not been chosen for your human heritage but for your spirit of repentance and humility. My gifts can operate best through those who are willing to be cleansed and willing to be used to proclaim My Love.

SUNDAY   Hebrews 2:14-18

For because he himself has suffered and been tempted, he is able to help those who are tempted.   Hebrews 2:18

Do not forget that I, too, have suffered and been tempted, My child. By taking upon Myself your nature I have delivered you from bondage to the devil. Those who fear death have not yet realized the true meaning of the Resurrection, but you know Me as the One who has paid the price for your sins. There is no fear of death in those who *put their trust in Me.*

MONDAY   Ephesians 1:7

In him, we have redemption through his blood, the forgiveness of our trespasses, according to the riches of his grace. Ephesians 1:7

My Love is the greatest healing Power in the world. It heals bodies, minds, spirits, and souls that have been broken by the sins of others or by their own personal sins. My Blood was shed because My Father and I have loved—not because men were more powerful. I could have called for the protection of legions of angels and routed those who put Me to death on the Cross. But then the redemption of sinners would not have been possible. I died: to save *you*—each of you—from the destruction of sin.

TUESDAY   Isaiah 40:28-31

But they who wait for the Lord shall renew their strength, they shall mount up with wings like eagles, they shall run and not be weary, they shall walk and not faint.   Isaiah 40:31

You are going on a journey. It will be an errand of mercy. It will be tiring, but I will renew your strength. My compassion will flood you, and I will use you to channel My Love into those in need of healing. My gifts will be available for you as they are needed. You have nothing to fear, for I am preparing the hearts of those to whom you will speak. Listen only to Me. I know the needs and I will reveal them to you. You must not let false humility tempt you to run from this assignment. Let Me remove the excess baggage in your spirit as I prepare you —daily.

WEDNESDAY   Romans 12:21; I John 5:4-5

Do not be overcome by evil, but overcome evil with good. Romans 12:21

My daughter, I am pleased with what you have done, but there is much more for you to do. Do not hold back the fulfillment of My Plan for your life with your procrastination. Offer it to Me. Let Me overcome in you what you cannot do in or for yourself. The enemy will seek to delay you with many distractions. Claim the power of My Blood over each of the circumstances. You do not have to be a "defeated Christian." Live victoriously in My Power—today.

THURSDAY   I Corinthians 14:33

For God is not a God of confusion but of peace.   I Corinthians 14:33

Confusion is one of the devil's best weapons. When he can confuse you, he can delay My Will in your life. When he can get your eyes off Me, he can keep you so preoccupied with his devious whisperings that you will live fruitlessly. Keep centered in Me. When you are confused, offer the situation to Me and ask for clarification of My Will. Claim the power of My Blood over it. If this confusion is of Satan, it will then have to recede. My Light will dispel the darkness.

FRIDAY   Romans 12:1-2

Do not be conformed to this world but be transformed by the renewal of your mind, that you may prove what is the will of God, what is good and acceptable and perfect. Romans 12:2

Sometimes I have to allow you to become confused because you are so determined to go ahead of Me in your own strength and will. You are pulled by the world into patterns and pathways I never intended. Let Me remake your whole nature, not just the "religious" part of your life. Dedicate to Me the *whole* of your life: these neighbors you do not like, the parent you still fear or resent, the son or daughter you cannot easily love and enjoy, the mate you think needs to be remodeled. Let Me transform your whole attitude, your tastes and preferences, your family life. You cannot do this of yourself alone.

SATURDAY   Isaiah 2:11; I Corinthians 4:9-13

We are fools for Christ's sake, but you are wise in Christ. We are weak, but you are strong. You are held in honor, but we in disrepute.   I Corinthians 4:10

You have let your pride be hurt in this situation. Ask for My humility so that you can see it with My eyes. You have said that you would be willing to be made a fool for My sake. *Be* ready to take the less glorious way if I call you there. Be patient as you fill the "night shift" instead of the seats of honor that would glorify you. Let Me teach you selfless humility through this experience of pain. It will not be wasted.

SUNDAY   Ephesians 4:26-27; James 1:19-22

For the anger of man does not work the righteousness of God.   James 1:20

You are too prone to claim this problem of quick anger as your temperament: to say that it cannot be changed. Let Me transform the old carnal nature in you. Let Me cut you free from the bondages of the past that Satan uses to make you react in anger in the present situation. You are responding in hostility because of an earlier hurt. I know *all* of your past.

With the sword of My Spirit I am now cutting you free from the person who caused such violent anger in your inner child of the past. I now cast this possessive spirit of anger out of you. My Love is now healing this buried memory. Give it *entirely* to Me.

MONDAY   James 1:2-4; St. John 14:18

I will not leave you desolate; I will come to you.   St. John 14:18

You are still the dawdling child in some areas of your life. This child grew up in fear of censure from a perfectionist parent or teacher. If something could be put off, the day of reckoning would be postponed. This hidden child of the past is still dominating your adult life, making you postpone doing things you are afraid that you may not do well. Let Me heal memories of the undeveloped part of you that is afraid of failure. In My Love this child of the past can now grow up into a mature person who does not have to procrastinate. Pray for My grace— then let Me do in and through you what you cannot do alone!

TUESDAY   Ephesians 4:22-24; Romans 8:37-39

And put on the new nature, created after the likeness of God in true righteousness and holiness.   Ephesians 4:24

My child, you are cringing in fear of this problem in your life. As a child of the King you have My limitless resources available to you for the asking and claiming. I cannot give you what you will not accept because of memories of fearful periods in your past life. The old man in you is dead. Now let My

Light and Love flow back into these dark areas of memory to open all the sealed doors and air out the dusty rooms in the house of life. Let the cringing inner child of the past come out of the closet to be healed so that you can grow in trust and obedience to My Will.

WEDNESDAY   Romans 13:11-14; Galatians 5:19-21

But put on the Lord Jesus Christ, and make no provision for the flesh, to gratify its desires.   Romans 13:14

You are letting the enemy poison your mind with jealousy. No one else can take the place I have appointed for you. You have given Me your life. I need you and many other workers also. Do not waste your energies in competition with others. Jealousy is a monster which will poison the whole of your life and destroy your effectiveness to serve Me—if you let it possess you as you have been doing. Let Me direct your life. Give this other person to Me now. When you truly make this surrender, new power will flow through you for the work I have called you to do.

THURSDAY   I Peter 1:3-9

In this you rejoice, though now for a little while you may have to suffer various trials, so that the genuineness of your faith, more precious than gold which though perishable is tested by fire, may redound to praise and glory and honor at the revelation of Jesus Christ.   I Peter 1:6-7

Wallowing in self-pity has been one of the tricks the enemy has used in the past to deceive you and destroy your spirit. He is attacking you again but you need not fall into his trap. You are My beloved child and I can protect you from this wasteful attitude if you call upon the power of My Blood *now*. Do this at once at the first thought of self-pity that knocks at the door of your mind. Send a wave of gratitude against the enemy. Let Me answer that Satanic knock. In praise and thanksgiving let Me take possession of your heart.

FRIDAY   James 1:5-8

> *But let him ask in faith, with no doubting, for he who doubts is like a wave of the sea that is driven and tossed by the wind.*   James 1:6

You have approached Me concerning these pressing needs in your life—but with doubt. You are to come in *believing* prayer, not doubting that I will answer. You have been double-minded—canceling your verbal prayers with the doubts and fears in your heart. The prayer of faith is much more than wishful thinking, much more than hopefulness. Claim My Power to bind these doubts and cast them out of your mind. Ask for My Light to shine in your heart to illumine the murky areas of doubt. Then claim My Promises and stand upon My Words in faith.

SATURDAY   Isaiah 30:15; Psalm 139:13-18

> *How precious to me are thy thoughts, O God! How vast is the sum of them!*   Psalm 139:17

I have a purpose for you that is beyond your understanding or your natural talents. I will open up the way when the time is ripe. You have been straining too hard, trying to accomplish too much. Your striving is futile. It is the enemy's way. My prophecy for you is for the distant future. You will be ready for it to be fulfilled in you only if you let Me choose the pattern for each of your days. I am quietly preparing you for this new work of healing. As your own memories of the painful past are being healed, you are growing toward this ministry. I am leading the way. *Trust in Me.*

SUNDAY   Romans 11:33-36

O the depth of the riches and wisdom and knowledge of God! How unsearchable are his judgments and how in-scrutable his ways!   Romans 11:33

My ways are higher than your ways. When you cannot see the reason, trust in Me to make it clear in My own way and time. I know your *deepest* needs, not just your superficial needs. I am changing your circumstances and attitudes as fast as you will let Me. Lift this disappointment and leave it with Me. When I close a door it is because I will open a better one—when you are ready. Let Me *use* this frustration. Let Me take the sting out of it. *Bask in My Love* for you—not the love of others. My Love changes not!

MONDAY   James 1:16-17,25; Ephesians 4:22-24

Every good endowment and every perfect gift is from above, coming down from the Father of lights with whom there is no variation or shadow due to change.   James 1:17

My Father yearns to bestow on you every good and per-fect gift. His Love for you never varies. He has predestined you to be a new kind of creature, one who is reborn out of old angers, malice, lusts of the past. But you must *act* upon this message and *accept* the free gift of life lived in His victorious Power. This is the law that sets you free from the old you of the past. *Claim* this gift of new life. Act upon it. Open the wrappings of the gift and put on this new garment of Love. *Accept* His Love as your way of life.

TUESDAY   Deuteronomy 30:15-20

If you obey the commandments of the Lord your God which I command you this day, by loving the Lord your God, by walking in his ways, and by keeping his commandments and his statutes and his ordinances, then you shall live and multiply, and the Lord your God will bless you in the land which you are entering to take possession of it. Deuteronomy 30:16

You are about to enter a new land. If you keep centered in My Will and in My Love, you shall be blessed and shall take possession of it in My Name. But if you turn to worship false gods, your hopes will fade and your strength will be dissipated. My victory can be won only by those who are single-minded, obedient to My commands. Walk in My Light today.

WEDNESDAY   Hebrews 13:20-21

Now may the God of peace who brought again from the dead our Lord Jesus, the great shepherd of the sheep, by the blood of the eternal covenant, equip you with everything good that you may do his will, working in you that which is pleasing in his sight, through Jesus Christ; to whom be glory for ever and ever. Amen. Hebrews 13:20-21

I am your Master and Lord of the flock that you have been tending. Fear not to leave it now to Me. I have need of you elsewhere, but I will not let these sheep stray away in your absence. My sheep hear My Voice. I am calling you to a higher pasture where the demands will be greater. My strength will be available to you in your weakness. Trust in Me to bring forth through you what you cannot possibly accomplish in your own wisdom and strength alone. I lead the way.

THURSDAY James 5:19-20

My brethren, if any one among you wanders from the truth and some one brings him back, let him know that whoever brings back a sinner from the error of his way will save his soul from death and will cover a multitude of sins. James 5:19-20

One of your companions on the way has fallen into the trap of the enemy. He has strayed from the truth but you are not to condemn him. You are to be My patient intercessor for his soul—even as I have been patient in interceding for yours. Claim My victory in his life no matter what the circumstances. In believing prayer, take the sword of My Spirit and cut him free from the bondage to those who would lead him astray. Claim the Power of My Blood over him and bind and cast out the spirit of deceit in him. Draw him in love into My Light.

FRIDAY St. Matthew 6:33-34

Therefore do not be anxious about tomorrow, for tomorrow will be anxious for itself. Let the day's own trouble be sufficient for the day. St. Matthew 6:34

Your life has been too scattered of late. You are seeking the Kingdom but not putting it *first* in your life. You have let

Satan tempt you with good works that are not My *highest* Plan. He can keep you very busy—so busy that you are tense and hurried. Relax in Me this minute. Give Me the rest of the day. Do only those things that I give you to do. Leave the rest to Me. I will supply their needs through other channels. You are not indispensable. Look only to Me for each decision. It matters what I think—not what others think. Stay centered in Me. Rest in Me.

SATURDAY   James 1:19-22,26; St. Matthew 12:34-37

The good man out of his good treasure brings forth good, and the evil man out of his evil treasure brings forth evil. St. Matthew 12:35

Have you spoken sharply in malice this week? Let me take control over your tongue and put My words in the place of those cutting ones you used yesterday. Do not deceive yourself. Your good works and religious observances are futile if the tongue is full of malice. The fruit of My Spirit are love, peace, patience, kindness, goodness, faithfulness, joy, humility, self-control. Your religious professions are false if My fruit do not show in your life. Your own tongue is your worst accuser. Give it to Me to be bridled in My Love.

SUNDAY   James 1:12-14

Let no one say when he is tempted, "I am tempted by God"; for God cannot be tempted with evil and he himself tempts no one; but each person is tempted when he is lured and enticed by his own desire.   James 1:13-14

You have said that I tempted you, but this is not true. The devil tempts you to sin. He entices you to listen to sinful thoughts and insinuations which come at you; but you need not give them room in your heart. Whether it is lust or fear or resentment or self-pity, you need not be led into sin if you will resist the first thoughts and claim the power of My Blood over them. The longer you dally with the thoughts, the easier will be Satan's victory. You are a child of God protected by My shed blood—*if you claim it!*

MONDAY Jeremiah 17:7-10

Blessed is the man who trusts in the Lord, whose trust is the Lord.   Jeremiah 17:7

My child, you have been deceived in your heart by the enemy who is always seeking to discourage and confuse. You are not thinking My thoughts after Me. You are confusing the issues. My wisdom is often foolishness to those who do not know Me. But you do know Me, and Satan can have no part in you when you walk in My Light. Do not listen to his false insinuations of fear and weariness. He cannot deceive My children if they claim My Power over each decision or situation. Do not wait for his attack—claim My Wisdom in advance.

TUESDAY St. John 14:23-24

Jesus answered him, "If a man loves me, he will keep my word, and my Father will love him, and we will come to him and make our home with him." St. John 14:23

You have been obedient in many areas but you are still lacking in understanding of the part My *discipline* must play in your spiritual growth. Express your love for Me not only in words of praise and adoration but also in *obedience*. My Father and I will abide in you as you listen and obey these commands that are for your own good. You are too often arguing—dissipating your energies. When you obey, you feel My Peace in your heart. Why do you so often delay? In My Will *is* your Peace.

WEDNESDAY   I Thessalonians 5:15-18

Rejoice always, pray constantly, give thanks in all circumstances; for this is the will of God in Christ Jesus for you. I Thessalonians 5:16-18

My child, you are very faithful in remembering the Sabbath day to keep it holy. But you often forget to keep your weekdays as holy. I am concerned with *all* of your life—not just certain hours or days or aspects or observances or rites! Keep Me in the center of your life by looking to Me often throughout each day. Pray quick "word prayers" for help or patience or thanksgiving during the midst of the daily routine. I have promised to be with you *always*—not just on Sundays.

THURSDAY   St. Matthew 28:20

And lo, I am with you always, to the close of the age. St. Matthew 28:20b

The years ahead will be more fruitful because you are learning to trust in Me and not in your own resources. You have much to learn, much to receive from Me. The inner Peace you are experiencing is a fruit of My indwelling Spirit. Your security is in *Me* not in others. You need not fear what they will think. Keep your will surrendered to My Will. Look to Me for guidance at each turning of the road. The way may be steep at times but My staff will comfort you. I am with you *always!*

FRIDAY   Malachi 3:10-12

Bring the full tithes into the storehouse, that there may be food in my house; and thereby put me to the test, says the Lord of hosts, if I will not open the windows of heaven for you and pour down for you an overflowing blessing. Malachi 3:10

My child, I will pour out a blessing upon you that will encompass you and your whole family. The enemy has been assaulting you, but I will rebuke the devourer for your fruit shall not be destroyed. Prove Me. *Believe Me* when you pray and it shall be done. Your prayers of thanksgiving open the way for Me to reach your loved ones. Continue faithful—in prayers of thanksgiving, not in criticism or fear.

SATURDAY   St. Mark 8:34-38

For whoever would save his life will lose it; and whoever loses his life for my sake and the gospel's will save it. St. Mark 8:35

You have much to learn about losing your life to save it. You have been self-centered and often your own worst enemy. Trust Me with your life and your livelihood. If you gain wealth at the expense of others you will be losing your own soul. Be honest in all your dealings—your bills and taxes, your relationships with fellow workers and those who work for you. They, too, are My children.

SUNDAY   Romans 12; St. John 15:9-11

Love one another with brotherly affection; outdo one another in showing honor.   Romans 12:10

My child, you are fearful of becoming involved lest I might ask too much of you—your time, energies, money. Your commitment stops short of involvement with people and their needs. The incarnation was My total involvement with you, with the whole world—not just for one brief span of thirty-three years but for eternity. My involvement is with you as a voter, a parent, an employee, a sinner who is called to be a saint, a member of the household of God. Let Me show you areas where you need to be more involved for your own spiritual growth—not just to help others. Examine your life fearlessly, humbly, honestly—in My Love let it be judged so that it may become healed. In My Will there is joy that you cannot conceive of until you become involved and experience My Joy in you—and *through you* to meet the needs of others!

MONDAY   St. Mark 4:21-25; St. John 1:1-13

For there is nothing hid, except to be made manifest; nor is anything secret, except to come to light.   St. Mark 4:22

Some of you have said that you could not share your vision and knowledge of Me with others because it was "too personal" or "too precious." But you are mistaken. This is *your purpose* as bearers of My Name—not just to receive for yourselves but *to share My Love with others*. Why do you imagine that you can truly share Me if you are too bound up in yourselves to speak a word of witness to others? You are to be a candle to light the Way for those in present darkness— mental, emotional, physical, spiritual. You do not light a candle in your home and put it under the bed. I am the Light of the World and you are called in your vow as a Christian to be a Lightbearer—to let My Light within you shine forth to brighten the world about you. There is much darkness, but My Light overcomes the darkness.

TUESDAY   Ephesians 5:8-17, 23; St. John 8:12

For once you were darkness, but now you are light in the Lord; walk as children of light.   Ephesians 5:8

My children, you are My Body. You are the Church of which I am Head. My ministers of reconciliation can be farm- ers or fishermen, homemakers or business executives, teachers or doctors. If your home and your work have been dedicated to Me, then you are called to be a minister of reconciliation right where you are *NOW*—not in some far distant place. Some of you are called to the ordained ministry but *ALL* of you are called to show forth My Light. If My Light is truly in you, there will be a quality about your life that will draw others to you—and then through you to *Me!*

WEDNESDAY   I Peter 5:7; Ephesians 6:18

Pray at all times in the Spirit, with all prayer and supplica- tion. To that end keep alert with all perseverance, making supplication for all the saints.   Ephesians 6:18

You are going through a tunnel of pain and grief for the situations and persons around you. How much greater is My grief for them! Let your spirit reach up to Me and then out to these others. *In union with Me* your prayers for them will be more effective. Your desires for them will be channeled in My directions—not your own! Put all these burdens on Me and I will give you rest. Let go and let Me take this responsibility that weighs so heavily on your heart. You cannot lift their loads for them. But *through you* (as you abide in Me) I can lift these persons into My greater Reality and situations will change. Pray for them in the Spirit, letting My Spirit—in union with yours—pray through you.

THURSDAY   St. John 14:10-12

Truly, truly, I say to you, he who believes in me will also do the works that I do; and greater works than these will he do, because I go to the Father.   St. John 14:12

When you are in union with Me, your own desires are dissolved in Mine. In this deep inner stillness your spirit is merged with Mine. You and the Father and I are *ONE*—your spirit reaching to Us as We reach down to you in creative, silent oneness. Be still and *KNOW My Peace.*

FRIDAY   St. John 15:9-11; Colossians 1:26-27

As the Father has loved me, so have I loved you; abide in my love.   St. John 15:9

Each day open yourself to Me in this creative union of contemplation. *Rest in Me*—your body, mind and spirit resting in Me. I am in you—your hope of glory. Glory in these times of silent adoration. Abide in Me. Let My Joy fill your heart.

SATURDAY   St. John 12:31-32; 6:36-40

And I, when I am lifted up from the earth, will draw all men to myself.   St. John 12:32

As you ask for My Presence to enter into you today in this deep stillness, a layer of Peace is being formed within you so that the irritations and frustrations of the day cannot get through to hurt your spirit. Let yourself be drawn into Me, and then ask for My Will to be done in others. As their names or needs float into your mind let them not be an intrusion but an instant effortless lifting of their spirits to Me. *Draw them into Me*—not yourself! Much more is accomplished through this kind of prayer than you can imagine.

SUNDAY   Deuteronomy 4:29-31; St. Luke 10:27

But from there you will seek the Lord your God, and you will find him, if you search after him with all your heart and with all your soul.   Deuteronomy 4:29

I am the Lord your God and I will not fail you. Today the going will be rough; but as you center in Me now, I am *in you* to strengthen you. Rest in Me now before the daily testings begin. In quietness and confident trust in Me will be your strength. My Love is filling you NOW—brimful, overflowing, spilling out to meet the needs of others whom you will encounter. Accept each one in My holy Love. See each one with My Wisdom. Unless you love Me with all your heart, soul, strength, and mind, you will not be able to love your neighbor. You will not even be able to love (accept) yourself. My *first commandment is to love Me.* Then My Love will enable you to accept yourself without self-condemnation, but in honesty. When you *know* in your heart, mind, and soul that *I love you just as you are,* then you will not have to criticize others to justify yourself: you will be able to *love them as yourself.*

MONDAY   Psalm 125:1-3

Those who trust in the Lord are like Mount Zion, which cannot be moved, but abides for ever.   Psalm 125:1

Fear not, My child, the works of darkness—for My arms are round about you like the mountains encircling Jerusalem. The enemy's scepter cannot rest upon you, for you have put your trust in Me, and I have established you in righteousness according to My Will for your life. You are protected as you continue to trust in Me. Abide in Me.

TUESDAY   Psalm 121

The Lord will keep your going out and your coming in from this time forth and for evermore.   Psalm 121:8

Trust in Me to keep you safe by day or by night. You have committed your life to Me. Know that My promises are true. I am faithful and just to keep My Word. Lift up your eyes to Me this morning. Take them off the day's problems and uncertainties. Be certain of My Love; be sure of My Protection. I will keep you from all evil. I will watch over your life.

WEDNESDAY   I Corinthians 11:23-26

For as often as you eat this bread and drink the cup, you proclaim the Lord's death until he comes.   I Corinthians 11:26

When you partake of My Body and Blood under the forms of the bread and wine as I have commanded you to do, remember that you are proclaiming My death until I return. This spiritual transfusion is available to you by faith. As you accept this new covenant with thanksgiving, you are to recall My death—My sacrificial Love for you personally. Receive Me—receive *Me* joyously under the forms used to recall My Presence.

THURSDAY   Romans 8:11; I Corinthians 10:16-17

If the Spirit of him who raised Jesus from the dead dwells in you, he who raised Christ Jesus from the dead will give life to your mortal bodies also through his Spirit which dwells in you.   Romans 8:11

As you receive Me in the breaking of bread, remember that you are being transfused by My Spirit. The Father who raised Me from the dead is giving new life to your mortal bodies. Claim My promise as you partake at Holy Communion of the consecrated elements. Know that they are vehicles for

My transforming, healing Power to flow into you—to quicken and heal you.

FRIDAY I Corinthians 11:27-31

Let a man examine himself, and so eat of the bread and drink of the cup. I Corinthians 11:28

When you obey My command to eat the bread and drink the cup of the new covenant, you act as part of My Body the Church. If you come prepared in humility to examine yourself and confess your sins, you will go away with the great blessing of joy—of forgiveness received. There is healing in My Blood —healing for your body as well as your mind and spirit and soul. There is cleansing for all who drink in repentance—in a manner worthy of My sacrifice.

SATURDAY I Corinthians 12:26-27

If one member suffers, all suffer together; if one member is honored, all rejoice together. I Corinthians 12:26

Have you grieved in another's grief and borne with him his suffering today? Have you rejoiced with one who has been preferred above you today? My Body has many members, *each one* individually a part of My Plan. You are called to be a part of this Body and to manifest these new gifts I have given you for the building up of the Church. Whatever you think or say or do, let it be to the glory of God—not to your own glory.

SUNDAY   I Corinthians 12:31-13:3

If I give away all I have, and if I deliver my body to be burned, but have not love, I gain nothing.   I Corinthians 13:3

My gifts are given to you to be used in the *way* of Love. No matter how great they are, unless you use them in My Way of Love they will be of no real value. You are to seek My supernatural gifts but only so that they will proclaim My Love to others. Seek earnestly these higher gifts because you *love* the brethren and want to be a channel of ministry to their needs.

MONDAY   I Corinthians 13:13-14:1

Make love your aim, and earnestly desire the spiritual gifts, especially that you may prophesy.   I Corinthians 14:1

My child, you have been given this gift for the edification of others. Prophesy to My people of My Love. There are many who cannot hear My Voice calling them to deeper commitment and wider service. Too many are content with serving Me in their own petty, natural strength. Prophesy in faith and hope to them, but let Love always be your aim.

TUESDAY   Proverbs 16:3,9

Commit your work to the Lord, and your plans will be established.   Proverbs 16:3

You have planned your ways, but I have directed your steps. Trust Me in the little details of each day to strengthen your faith. Commit to Me your work, your family, the one you love the most. Commit your problems as well as your relationships. Let Me take this burden from your shoulders. Let Me show you how this seemingly impossible task can be accomplished. Let Me establish your work so that the enemy cannot destroy it.

WEDNESDAY   Psalm 91:13-15

When he calls to me, I will answer him; I will be with him in trouble, I will rescue him and honor him.   Psalm 91:15

Because you have remained faithful to Me in love, I will deliver you from this attack of the enemy. He has no power over those who call upon the protection of My Name. I will rescue you and guide you out of this difficulty, for you have called upon Me in faith. Your adversaries will have no power over you. You will trample underfoot Satan's efforts to distract you. Victory will be Mine in your life.

THURSDAY   Psalm 91:9-12

Because you have made the Lord your refuge, the Most High your habitation, no evil shall befall you, no scourge come near your tent.   Psalm 91:9-10

I have given My angels charge over you to bear you up in this situation. They have guarded you from the attacks of the enemy because you have claimed My Power in each trial.

You have been under fire because you have put your trust in Me. Continue in My Power. Walk in My Love. No evil shall destroy My work through you.

FRIDAY   Psalm 139:1-6,13

O Lord, thou hast searched me and known me! Psalm 139:1

My child, I have known you from your mother's womb. My hand has been upon you. I have known all your innermost thoughts. Do not try to hide this secret sin from Me. You cannot hide from My Spirit. My Knowledge of you is complete. Offer this sin to Me and let Me redeem it. Offer this lust to Me so that I can purify your body as well as your spirit. The carnal man is lusting against the spirit. Let Me claim this victory in you.

SATURDAY   Psalm 136:1-9

O give thanks to the Lord, for he is good, for his stead-fast love endures for ever. Psalm 136:1

I have made the earth and the waters, the sun and moon and stars in the heavens. And do you not think, son of man, that I can heal you? My steadfast Love endures forever. Give thanks for My Love and for the wonders of My Grace. My Mercy endures forever in the lives of those who put their trust in Me. Give thanks without ceasing. Rest in My healing, recreating Love, and wait for My wonders to be revealed in you.

SUNDAY Colossians 1:26-27

To them God chose to make known how great among the Gentiles are the riches of the glory of this mystery, which is Christ in you, the hope of glory. Colossians 1:27

Your hope of glory is in Me, My child—not in your own strivings. I have called you to this ministry of prayer, and your intercessions will be joined with Mine. There are many who need to know this secret. They are scattered all around you. Let Me open your eyes to see their deepest needs. Claim My Presence in them—not the enemy's. See them with My eyes—*see Me* in each one of them.

MONDAY Colossians 1:24-26

Now I rejoice in my sufferings for your sake, and in my flesh I complete what is lacking in Christ's afflictions for the sake of his body, that is, the church. Colossians 1:24

You are one of those whom I have chosen to be a messenger—to announce this secret, the Good News of My abiding, indwelling Presence. This is bearing the Cross, for there will be persecutions and rejections ahead. Are you willing to be a servant in the Church? Will you give up the seats of honor and take the lowly role of messenger? Will you proclaim My Love in all your attitudes, in all your relationships?

TUESDAY James 4:7

Submit yourselves therefore to God. Resist the devil and he will flee from you. James 4:7

Submission is not easy for you, My child. You are still trying to have your own way in this matter. The devil is tempting you to pull away from My Will. He is distracting you with worldly idols. This restlessness is not of Me. Turn back and submit your life to Me. Be willing to be whatever I call you to be. Let not fear of the future hold back your submission. *Resist* the enemy. My perfect Love casts out fear. Claim My Love in this situation and the enemy will flee from you.

WEDNESDAY II Timothy 1:7

For God did not give us a spirit of timidity but a spirit of power and love and self-control. II Timothy 1:7

I have not given you a spirit of fear but of My Power. In My Love you will be able to love this one who seems to you to be unlovable. Claim this Love. Act upon it. Be loving. Let Me heal your memories of past hurts, of times when your feelings were trampled upon, when you felt rejected. Let Me bind and cast out this spirit of rejection. Your mind is *now* being healed of these painful memories as My Light shines in the darkness of the past. *Be made whole!*

THURSDAY   St. Luke 8:43-48

And he said to her, "Daughter, your faith has made you well; go in peace."   St. Luke 8:48

My daughter, you have touched the hem of My garment and you will never be the same. You are changing slowly but surely, turning from the superficial ways of the world to My Way of Life and Truth. I am wooing your spirit that you may be made whole in My Love. Your faith has made the contact with My infinite healing Power. Rejoice and *accept your healing now!*

FRIDAY   Romans 12:2

Do not be conformed to this world but be transformed by the renewal of your mind, that you may prove what is the will of God, what is good and acceptable and perfect.   Romans 12:2

Obedience is a sign of your love for Me. When you are conforming yourself to the values and standards of the world, you are not conforming yourself to My higher ways. Let Me transform your life. Let Me release My Love in each relationship. Let My Power flow through you to meet the needs of others. Begin today, right where you are—*now.*

SATURDAY   St. Luke 8:19-21

But he said to them, "My mother and my brothers are those who hear the word of God and do it."   St. Luke 8:21

You were lonely but I have given you a new family. Your new mother and brothers and sisters are those who listen for

My Voice and heed My warnings. With them you will find rich fellowship. They may be of many ages, races, denominations, and nationalities—but you will feel that they are your family because they love and obey My Word. You will share My love with a very large family that extends around the world.

SUNDAY   St. Luke 9:59-62

Jesus said to him, "No one who puts his hand to the plow and looks back is fit for the kingdom of God."   St. Luke 9:62

You have been called to a deeper ministry to this larger family. When I call you, you must follow without looking back. You have put your hand to the plow and there is much work to be done. The ground in the hearts of those about you must be well tilled before the seeds of the Kingdom are deeply planted. There is no turning back for those who commit their lives to bringing in My Kingdom. No excuses, no procrastinations are now valid. You cannot stand still any longer. You must go forward. Follow Me.

MONDAY   I Corinthians 10:31

So, whether you eat or drink, or whatever you do, do all to the glory of God.   I Corinthians 10:31

Are you doing these things in the Church for My glory or for your own? Ask yourself this question each time you take on a new responsibility. Is your life being lived to please others or to glorify Me? Does your overeating glorify Me— or is it a sign of your insecurity? Are you stumbling anyone else by your personal habits? Ask *Me* what to do. *Listen.* Obey!

TUESDAY   I Corinthians 10:13

No temptation has overtaken you that is not common to man. God is faithful, and he will not let you be tempted beyond your strength, but with the temptation will also provide the way of escape, that you may be able to endure it.   I Corinthians 10:13

When you are tempted, remember that you can call upon Me for strength to overcome. My Wisdom will show you the way of Victory if you call upon Me. Do not despair because there are many temptations. I, too, was tempted in the wilderness. I will not let the enemy overcome you if you look to Me for help and stand firm in the power of My Victory. Claim My Blood over every temptation. I died for *you*.

WEDNESDAY   Acts 7:54-60

And he knelt down and cried with a loud voice, "Lord, do not hold this sin against them." And when he had said this, he fell asleep.   Acts 7:60

Do not become bitter, My child, because of those who have turned against you to persecute you. The jealousy of cruel men crucified Me. Like Stephen the martyr you have been stoned by these lies, but you have not been put to death.

Can you pray as he did that their sins not be held against them? Can you forgive those who persecute you? Let Me win the victory as you forgive them for their sins. Your resentments will hurt you—not them. A bitter heart poisons your whole body. Forgive. *Want* to forgive *as I forgive!*

THURSDAY   St. Matthew 25:31-46

And the King will answer them, "Truly, I say to you, as you did it to one of the least of these my brethren, you did it to me."   St. Matthew 25:40

Give this one who has hurt you a cup of water in My Name. Remember that whatever you do to him you are doing unto Me. In turning the other cheek you will win him to Me. My Love will enable you to *be* Love in this difficult situation. It is not as hopeless as you think. My Love avails much. Forgive him—even as I have forgiven you.

FRIDAY   Amos 5:24

But let justice roll down like waters, and righteousness like an everflowing stream.   Amos 5:24

My justice is sufficient for you. My righteousness will be like an ever-flowing stream. A forgiving heart is a greater sacrifice to Me than burnt offerings. My justice cannot be evaded: it will roll down like waters. Let Me bring good out of this situation as you forgive the one who has hurt you. Judgment is Mine—not yours.

SATURDAY II Chronicles 7:14

If my people who are called by my name humble them-
selves, and pray and seek my face, and turn from their
wicked ways, then I will hear from heaven, and will for-
give their sin and heal their land. II Chronicles 7:14

You are concerned about today's sinful world, but you
have not cared enough to humble yourself and pray. You are
a part of the sin of this world. Pray for the wickedness to be
revealed and repented of by each sinner. Pray and seek My
face in fasting. In the early morning silence, pray th·t the
sinful will turn from their wicked ways. I have promised to
forgive their sin and heal their land. Pray and seek My Will.

SUNDAY I Corinthians 13:4

Love is patient and kind; love is not jealous or boastful.
I Corinthians 13:4

You have been jealous again. Remember that no one else
can fulfill the place that has been prepared for you if you
walk in My Love. You must be patient so that My plans for
you can unfold. In kindness to all, in humility (not boastful-
ness), you will find a new Peace in your life. When you live
in a spirit of My Love, there is no room for jealousy.

MONDAY I Corinthians 13:5

It is not arrogant or rude. Love does not insist on its own
way; it is not irritable or resentful. I Corinthians 13:5

When you are irritable and impatient, it is really because
you are letting the old carnal nature revive. You are thinking

of self, preoccupied with your own plans and interests. Give
Me this episode. Ask My forgiveness and that of the one you
have hurt with your rudeness. You will be surprised that it is
easier to do than you think. If you ask for My help, the way
to reconciliation will be made clear. I will open a pathway.

TUESDAY   I Corinthians 13:7

*Love bears all things, believes all things, hopes all things,
endures all things.*   I Corinthians 13:7

You say that you are tired of believing for this loved one's
salvation. I was weary, too, in the Garden of Gethsemane, yet
I took upon Myself the salvation of the world. I bore the sins
of the world. You are only asked to *bear with* this person.
You have endured much, but the end is in sight. Love him with
My creative Love that not only hopes but believes. Hold him
up to Me each day in expectant trust—in awareness of My
great Love for him and My transforming, redeeming Power.

WEDNESDAY   II Thessalonians 1:3-4

*We are bound to give thanks to God always for you,
brethren, as is fitting, because your faith is growing abundantly, and the love of every one of you for one another
is increasing.*   II Thessalonians 1:3

Your faith is growing daily through these testings which
I am giving you grace to overcome. I did not promise you a
life of ease but *a cross to bear with Me.* I, too, was persecuted
—far more than you—by the jealousy and anger and spiteful-

ness of others. Be steadfast in your faith and in your love one for another. My Church will be persecuted by the world, but I have overcome the world.

THURSDAY   II Thessalonians 2:1-10

And then the lawless one will be revealed, and the Lord Jesus will slay him with the breath of his mouth and destroy him by his appearing and his coming.   II Thessalonians 2:8

You wonder at the spirit of rebellion and lawlessness that is possessing mankind. You cringe at the false prophets and heresies that have entered even into My Churches at times. I warned you that this would be so in the last days when the prince of this world would make his last attempt to seduce and destroy the spirits of men. But when I return in power, I will destroy the works of the enemy, and you shall be lifted up with Me in glory—you who remain faithful to Me, who love the Truth, and who put all your trust in Me shall be saved.

FRIDAY   II Thessalonians 2:11-15

So then, brethren, stand firm and hold to the traditions which you were taught by us, either by word of mouth or by letter.   II Thessalonians 2:15

You have refused to take on the unrighteousness of the world and its false gods and perverted signs and wonders. You are being sanctified by My indwelling Spirit, the Holy Comforter, whom I have sent to lead you into all Truth, to strengthen your witness. Continue to *hold steadfastly to My promises* so that you may be with Me in glory when that awefull day of My return comes.

SATURDAY II Thessalonians 2:16-3:5

May the Lord direct your hearts to the love of God and to the steadfastness of Christ. II Thessalonians 3:5

Pray for the brethren who are under persecution in other countries, that they may be comforted and strengthened by My Grace. Pray for yourself that you may be able to resist the temptations when they come and may be delivered from evil men and machinations of the devil. Pray for My Love to comfort you, My Grace to make you steadfast. Pray for all who have not faith enough to believe in My return that is drawing nigh.

SUNDAY St. Matthew 28:20; II Thessalonians 3:3-5

But the Lord is faithful; he will strengthen you and guard you from evil. II Thessalonians 3:3

No matter how much the devil unleashes his evil power in the world about you, there is nothing for you to fear if you remain steadfast in My Love. I have promised to be with you *always*—to the very close of the age. I will direct your comings and goings. I will protect you from the evil one. I will keep you strong in My Love as you put your trust in Me and obey My Will for your life. I will be with you in Power and inward Peace.

MONDAY I Thessalonians 5:19-22

But test everything; hold fast what is good, abstain from every form of evil.   I Thessalonians 5:21-22

Do not believe all that you read or hear. Test the spirits of those who prophesy. If their words are truly of Me, you will know the witness (confirmation) of My Spirit in your heart. Do not quench My Spirit. Let My gifts flow freely through you in Love to meet the needs of My Body the Church. Remove from your life any hindrances, any dependencies that are not of Me. Hold firmly to whatever is good and pure in your thinking as well as in your speaking and doing.

TUESDAY I Thessalonians 5:23-24

May the God of peace himself sanctify you wholly; and may your spirit and soul and body be kept sound and blameless at the coming of our Lord Jesus Christ.   I Thessalonians 5:23

I have called you and I will sanctify you, but you have a part to play in this lifetime's work. You must be honest with yourself and with others. You must *will* to be made sanctified. Do not wait for Me to do the work: begin to *be* what I have called you to be—loving, forgiving, patient, full of faith. Feed on My Word—not your resentments or doubts or fears. Then *do what I would do* in this situation; and My Peace will enter into your mind and spirit and body.

WEDNESDAY   I Thessalonians 5:13-22

Be at peace among yourselves.   I Thessalonians 5:13b

Be at peace as brothers who will give hope to the discouraged, faith to the fainthearted. Do not retaliate against those who have done evil to you, but forgive them in patience. Return good for evil by praying constantly, by being loving in My Love to those who have been jealous of you. Their thoughts cannot harm you when you do not return condemnation but rather Love. Live in a spirit of continuous praise, and My Joy will be within you always, regardless of circumstances.

THURSDAY   I Thessalonians 5:12-13

But we beseech you, brethren, to respect those who labor among you and are over you in the Lord and admonish you.   I Thessalonians 5:12

Have no fear of those in authority over you, but hold them in respect as My instruments. If you are admonished, pray to know My Spirit confirming where there is truth. But be subject in humility to My Spirit that through the word of Wisdom you may know the truth about yourself. In honesty seek discernment that you may grow through this correction to be more usable by Me.

FRIDAY   I Thessalonians 5:8-11

For God has not destined us for wrath, but to obtain sal-
vation through our Lord Jesus Christ, who died for us so
that whether we wake or sleep we might live with him.
I Thessalonians 5:9-10

When you sleep at night, commit your spirit to Me. When
you awaken, commit your day to Me so that, asleep or awake,
My Spirit will abide within you. You are predestined for salvation: accept this *totally*—not just at certain moments of
exaltation. Put on the helmet (or hope) of salvation as you
awaken each morning. Wear the shield of faith each day.

SATURDAY   I Thessalonians 5:11

Therefore encourage one another and build one another
up, just as you are doing.   I Thessalonians 5:11

Your mission in life is to encourage others in the faith.
You are to build them up in My Love. Your words are to be
used to edify them, not to tear down My images of what they
can become. Hold carefully in faith these bundles I have
given you—they are very precious to Me. I have entrusted
them to you, not to be possessed by you, but to be loved by
Me through you. Beware of possessive love toward those I
have given you to love for Me.

SUNDAY   I Thessalonians 5:2-5

For you are all sons of light and sons of the day; we are
not of the night or of darkness.   I Thessalonians 5:5

The day of the Lord is coming when many who have dis-
owned Me will find themselves in great darkness. There is no

true security except in Me, no true peace except in My Peace. The world of evil will not hear My call, but you are sons and daughters of the Light. You need not fear the darkness, for you are not of darkness, but are children of Light. Walk in the Light. Be sober and vigilant against the deceitful wiles of the enemy. Be centered in Me—not in other human beings. Beware of idolatry of humans.

MONDAY I Samuel 15:23; 28:7-25; 31:6

For rebellion is as the sin of divination, and stubbornness is as iniquity and idolatry. Because you have rejected the word of the Lord, he has also rejected you from being king. I Samuel 15:23

There are those who have rejected My Word in this matter. They have been rebellious and stubborn and proud. Beware, lest you, too, cut yourself off from Me as King Saul did when he consulted the witch of Endor. Do not let a spirit of idolatry mislead you into sin. When you make a god of a human being, you lay yourself open to Satan's trap: he can deceive you through that person's weakness. No one is infallible. Be conformed to My Word, not to other people's standards or personalities or interpretations of My Word. Seek the gift of discernment of My Holy Spirit to lead you into all Truth. Test this in My Word.

TUESDAY Isaiah 61:3

To grant to those who mourn in Zion—to give them a garland instead of ashes, the oil of gladness instead of

mourning, the mantle of praise instead of a faint spirit;
that they may be called oaks of righteousness, the planting
of the Lord, that he may be glorified. Isaiah 61:3

Will you be an oak of righteousness of My planting? Or
will you bend like a willow before each storm? You have
mourned for a lost love. Let Me comfort you with My Love.
Let Me give you a garland instead of ashes and a mantle of
praise. Let Me anoint you with the oil of gladness instead of
ashes of mourning. Let me be glorified in your witness from
this day forward.

WEDNESDAY   Isaiah 66:1-2

Thus says the Lord: "Heaven is my throne and the earth
is my footstool; what is the house which you would build
for me, and what is the place of my rest?" Isaiah 66:1

Do not pride yourself on your fine churches and sanctu-
aries, for heaven is My throne. The earth is only My footstool.
I am not impressed by man's titles or accomplishments, but I
seek out the one who is humble and contrite in heart who
obeys My Word. *He* is the one whom I will use mightily!

THURSDAY   Jeremiah 1:5-8

But the Lord said to me, "Do not say, 'I am only a youth';
for to all to whom I send you you shall go, and whatever
I command you you shall speak." Jeremiah 1:7

Before you were formed in the womb, you were called
to serve Me. I have appointed you to be a prophet, and you

shall speak My words to all to whom I send you. Listen carefully for My still, small voice. Be not afraid to speak whatever words I command you, for I shall protect you and deliver you. Do not go ahead of Me. Wait upon My Spirit to move your lips. Wait upon Me with prayer and fasting; in praise and thanksgiving let your requests be made known to Me.

FRIDAY   Joshua 1:9

Have I not commanded you? Be strong and of good courage; be not frightened, neither be dismayed; for the Lord your God is with you wherever you go.   Joshua 1:9

Be not afraid of the new way I am preparing for you. My cup will be a cup of blessing, filled and running over. With the mercy you show to others, you will receive mercy. Be strong in My strength. Go forth in courage to be My instrument of grace to those in need. Trust only in Me. Go, for I am with you—wherever you go, I will be with you.

SATURDAY   Psalm 50:14-15

And call upon me in the day of trouble; I will deliver you, and you shall glorify me.   Psalm 50:15

You have not yet called upon Me in this problem, My child. You have been trying to do this work alone, and you have run into serious trouble. Be not afraid, for I will deliver you. You have turned back to Me now at last. Make your commitment to Me a vow that you will keep in thanksgiving, not out of duty. Delight to call upon Me. Want to glorify Me, *more than yourself.*

SUNDAY   Hebrews 6:11-12

And we desire each one of you to show the same earnest-
ness in realizing the full assurance of hope until the end,
so that you may not be sluggish, but imitators of those
who through faith and patience inherit the promises.   Hebrews 6:11-12

You have been earnestly proclaiming the hope of salvation to those who are still sluggish and lazy in their love for Me. Do not be discouraged by their lack of response. Continue to imitate those who inherit the promises of God. *Stand on My promises.* In patience, stand firm in the faith you have been given—faith in the Power of My Love to win them to Myself.

MONDAY   Isaiah 55:10-11

So shall my word be that goes forth from my mouth; it
shall not return to me empty, but it shall accomplish that
which I purpose, and prosper in the thing for which I
sent it.   Isaiah 55:11

I have given you My Word. Will you stand upon it? Will you claim it, not your pains and symptoms? Send My word of healing to every part of your body and *believe* that it will respond in healthy functioning according to its appointed plan. My Word shall not return to Me void. I have promised that it shall accomplish My purposes. Trust in Me.

TUESDAY   St. Luke 9:38-43

And all were astonished at the majesty of God.   St. Luke 9:43a

Are you amazed, My child, at the might of My Power? My hand is not shortened today. My Voice still commands the demons to depart from the spirits and bodies of those who are torn or convulsed by their attacks. This ministry is for those who are willing to pray and fast—those who will fast in their spirits from sin as well as in their bodies from food. It is My Will to heal many who are not healed yet because there is no one ready to claim My Power over the enemy today. Are you ready?

WEDNESDAY   Isaiah 55:8-9

For as the heavens are higher than the earth, so are my ways higher than your ways and my thoughts than your thoughts.   Isaiah 55:9

Do not be disturbed that things are not as you planned, My child. My ways are not your ways. My thoughts are higher than your thoughts. My miracles often come about silently in the hearts of men before they are seen by others. Be patient. Continue *perseveringly* in prayer. Keep your spirits high in praise and thanksgiving. Wait upon Me to bring forth My answer of healing in this relationship.

THURSDAY Philippians 4:19; St. Matthew 6:25

And my God will supply every need of yours according to his riches in glory in Christ Jesus. Philippians 4:19

When you become tense, rest in Me *at once.* Do not dally with any thoughts of weariness or self-pity. Do not criticize others or become impatient with them. Ask for and claim My Patience—My supply for all of your needs. I am concerned with *all* the details of your life. You need not be anxious if you stop at once to open the window of your spirit to the flooding of My Love.

FRIDAY Hebrews 13:5-6,8; Psalm 37:5-7

Jesus Christ is the same yesterday and today and for ever. Hebrews 13:8

You are reacting now to some painful memories of the past. Let My Light shine back through the years to dissolve these memories. Let My Love enfold each person, each circumstance. Commit *all* of your ways of the *past* to Me—not just the present or the future. Then I can better direct your paths according to My creative Will for your life.

SATURDAY Hebrews 13:14-16; Psalm 37:3-4

Take delight in the Lord, and he will give you the desires of your heart. Psalm 37:4

In the middle of each task, stop a moment to give thanks for its completion. Form a habit of praise, of expectancy. Let

My Light infiltrate your work to make it more creative. Let My Joy become your strength in each undertaking. Be more conscious of Me than of the difficulties in each situation. Face each day's tasks in My Power, in joyous expectancy, and in praise.

SUNDAY   Psalm 103:3,10-12; James 5:15-16

Therefore confess your sins to one another, and pray for one another, that you may be healed. The prayer of a righteous man has great power in its effects.   James 5:16

When you ask for My forgiveness, *claim it at once.* Remember that I love you enough to die for you—to make My grace available to you. The greater sin is to deny what My death has made available to you. To repent and confess is necessary—but having asked, *accept My forgiveness.* Let me wipe away the stings of guilt or remorse as My Blood cleanses your guilty memories and sets you free. I am now removing them as far as the East is from the West.

MONDAY   St. Luke 15:10,18-24; Ephesians 1:7-8

In him we have redemption through his blood, the forgiveness of our trespasses, according to the riches of his grace.   Ephesians 1:7

What are you waiting for, My child? I have given you the assurances of My forgiveness. Forgive yourself, and let Me erase this condemnation from the slate of life. The enemy is the accuser, the deceiver, the prince of lies. Do not listen to him, but listen to My words of healing forgiveness. My Love now sets you free. Claim it by faith—with joy! The angels rejoice with you now.

TUESDAY Romans 14:7-8,17-19; Galatians 6:2

Bear one another's burdens, and so fulfil the law of Christ.
Galatians 6:2

When you have let Me heal this completely, you will be used to proclaim My forgiveness, the Kingdom of God to others. What you have accepted for yourself, you will be able to give to others—the courage to believe that I have healed your brokenness and erased the marks and scars. The sting will be drawn and the pain will be turned to joy as you share My grace with others in need of My forgiveness.

WEDNESDAY St. Matthew 9:37-38; 10:1; II Corinthians 5:18-20

And he called to him his twelve disciples and gave them authority over unclean spirits, to cast them out, and to heal every disease and every infirmity. St. Matthew 10:1

My child, arise and go forth in My Light. I have fields for you to harvest. My Power will anoint your eyes to see as I see and your lips to speak as I speak My words through you. My healing Love is flowing deeply into you now—and through you to meet the needs of those whom you lift to me today. You are My channel to those I bring into your life. Fear not to give My healing, reconciling Love to others..

THURSDAY St. Matthew 11:28-30

Come to me, all who labor and are heavy laden, and I will give you rest. St. Matthew 11:28

You are not tired today because My Love has renewed your energies. This is the secret—to rest in Me for a few minutes between your tasks. Let Me renew your strength as you look to Me. Hand over your burdens to Me *often* throughout each day. Let no fearful or critical thought double the load. My Love is an enabling Power that will carry you through pressures without strain. Come to Me when you are weary and let Me refresh you.

FRIDAY Isaiah 30:15

For thus said the Lord God, the Holy One of Israel, "In returning and rest you shall be saved; in quietness and in trust shall be your strength." And you would not. Isaiah 30:15

My daughter, you have been under many pressures. Rest now in Me and let My Love renew your spirit. In quiet contemplation let My Spirit lead your spirit into new depths of Wisdom. You have been giving out much. Let Me now refill you. Enter into My silence—and rest. *Rest in Me.*

SATURDAY I Corinthians 3:5-9; I John 5:4-5

For whatever is born of God overcomes the world; and this is the victory that overcomes the world, our faith. I John 5:4

You have been used to plant many seeds that will spring up in the areas beyond your understanding. Water them with your prayers. Let the sunlight of My Love flood through you. Lift them to Me daily in thanksgiving, but do not try to measure their growth. Later you will see beautiful fruit. Leave the growing to Me. Do not try to harvest what you have planted. Release each one of them. Release them in joy. Victory is Mine.

SUNDAY   St. Matthew 8:24-27

And the men marveled, saying, "What sort of man is this, that even winds and sea obey him?"   St. Matthew 8:27

I have many purposes for the days ahead. Some of them will be dark days. Some will be stormy—but be not afraid. My Peace will abide in you in the midst of storms. You will be lifted over the waves. You will be carried through the darkness in Light that no man can quench. You have nothing to fear. Your faith will be strengthened by my Presence. Do not let your fears rock the boat. Be still and know.

MONDAY   Revelation 3:8-12

I am coming soon; hold fast what you have, so that no one may seize your crown.   Revelation 3:11

The new doorway that I am opening is not an easy one, but it will be rewarding. In the Spirit you will be led into deeper intercessions for those in need. I will teach you much that you have never learned, but it will not be for yourself alone. I know your innermost thoughts. You need only to pray to be kept in the center of My highest Will for your life.

TUESDAY   Ephesians 1:15-23; 4:1-7

I therefore, a prisoner for the Lord, beg you to lead a life worthy of the calling to which you have been called. Ephesians 4:1

I have new plans for your life. Some are beyond your furthest hopes. In obedient trust they will be fulfilled—but not by striving or straining. Let Me bring these opportunities for service in My timing. Be open. Be receptive. Be loving. Be expectant. Do joyously whatever I give you to do, no matter how small. *Be* My message to those about you.

WEDNESDAY   Psalm 100:4; Ephesians 1:4-6

He destined us in love to be his sons through Jesus Christ, according to the purpose of his will. Ephesians 1:5

Enter into My gates with thanksgiving. In praise make your needs known, and they shall be fulfilled. My Power is flowing through you now to those for whom you pray. My Power is life-changing. Fear not to trust your loved ones to Me. I love them more than you know. They are *My* children before they are yours. I have predestined them—before the foundation of the world—to be sons and daughters of God. Leave them to Me.

THURSDAY   Exodus 14:13-14; Psalm 40:1-4

The Lord will fight for you, and you have only to be still. Exodus 14:14

I know your loved ones' needs before you call upon Me. You need not beg—you need only to thank Me. Then stand still and watch My glorious Plans unfold in those for whom you pray. My answers will flow more freely when the channel is not blocked by fear or doubt or worry. Anxiety destroys your own effectiveness. Tension holds back the fulfillment of your prayers. Be patient. Wait upon Me.

FRIDAY   Colossians 1:9-14,19-20; James 4:7

Submit yourselves therefore to God. Resist the devil and he will flee from you.   James 4:7

When you are not getting through in a situation, claim My Blood over it. Know that My Power is greater than the enemy's. My Victory on the cross must be claimed to be effective in these situations where the enemy is trying to spoil or steal what he cannot win because of your faith. Be constant, steady in prayers of thanksgiving. The enemy hates these joyous prayers of resistance to his wiles.

SATURDAY   I John 1:7

But if we walk in the light, as he is in the light, we have fellowship with one another, and the blood of Jesus his Son cleanses us from all sin.   I John 1:7

In the fire of My Holiness, your sins have been consumed, My child. You have repented and asked My forgiveness. Accept My Joy through sins forgiven. Accept My grace to go and sin no more. I have purified your heart. No more shall you hold these secret guilts. They are washed away in the

Blood of the Lamb. I am glorified in your Joy as you go in praise and thanksgiving. Show forth My praise.

SUNDAY Psalm 97:10-12

Light dawns for the righteous, and joy for the upright in heart. Psalm 97:11

Because you love Me, you hate this evil attack that has come upon your Church. The enemy cannot prevail against those who love Me. Claim the delivering Power of My Blood. You hate the evil, but you must not hate the sinner. Pray against the devil's attack, but pray for deliverance of those who have allowed themselves to become his minions. I am preserving you from the hands of the ungodly. Rejoice.

MONDAY Psalm 98:7-9

He will judge the world with righteousness, and the peoples with equity. Psalm 98:9b

Do not fear these who worship the devil and try to persecute My people. They shall be confounded. As they sow evil, so they shall reap the evil of their ways. But *you* are not to judge them. I alone can judge, for I know the secrets of their hearts. I judge the world with righteousness and truth. They are part of the sin of the world, but you do not have to be a victim. Close your heart, mind, spirit, and soul to any thought-projections of others. Let My Holy Spirit filter out all impurities, all that is contrary to My Will.

TUESDAY Jeremiah 31:3; Psalm 23:4-6

I have loved you with an everlasting love; therefore I have continued my faithfulness to you. Jeremiah 31:3b

My child, I have loved you with an everlasting Love, and I have appointed you to bear much fruit. Fear not to go forth and do the works I have called you to do. The enemy has assaulted you through your loved ones, but you have nothing to fear. My rod and My staff strengthen you. I shall spread a table before you in the presence of your enemies. Your cup shall run over with My Joy. Goodness and mercy shall flow out of you, and you shall dwell in My Presence all the days of your life.

WEDNESDAY Jeremiah 31:12; St. Luke 19:17

And he said to him, "Well done, good servant! Because you have been faithful in a very little, you shall have authority over ten cities." St. Luke 19:17

I have set you in a watered garden where beauty abounds that your spirit may be refreshed by My creation. Accept all that I have given you in praise and thanksgiving, for my heart delights to give good gifts to My children. The sun shines on the just and on the unjust, but the bounty of My Love is reserved for those who, in obedience, abide in My Will. You have been faithful in little things, and I shall add more to them. Be faithful also in much.

THURSDAY   Colossians 1:13-14; Psalm 97:3;
                Psalm 91:3-6

He has delivered us from the dominion of darkness and transferred us to the kingdom of his beloved Son.   Colossians 1:13

When a spirit of deep weariness comes upon you, know that it is not from Me but from the enemy. Take dominion over this spirit in My Power and cast it out quickly. You need not allow the enemy to oppress you. With your first awakening thought each morning, claim a circle of My purifying fire around you.

FRIDAY   Isaiah 11:1-5; St. John 8:31-32

And you will know the truth, and the truth will make you free.   St. John 8:32

When you write this letter, pray that as My disciple you will be obedient. Know that My word will be written through you to set you free in this situation. The enemy has tried to trap you, but you are now free—free to be My instrument. You are to write in obedience as I have given you the words and as I will continue to give My wisdom in a spirit of prayer. And in My abiding Presence, the Truth which has set you free will be made known to others. In praise and thanksgiving, rest in Me.

SATURDAY   St. Luke 6:27-36; I Corinthians 13:1-13

But I say to you that hear, Love your enemies, do good to those who hate you.   St. Luke 6:27

Go on in this situation in My Love. When this one rejects you, remember that it is because he was once rejected. Pray for the little boy within the grown man to be set free. He is still hiding in dark shadows of hurt memories of loneliness and rejection. Give him now, as the grown man, more of My Love. I will take the sting of rejection out of you. I was once rejected by My earthly family too. Lift this one to Me daily in love.

SUNDAY   St. Luke 6:44-45; 4:18-19; 6:36

Be merciful, even as your Father is merciful.   St. Luke 6:36

I need to use you today on a special errand of mercy. There is one who has not been able to hear My words of Love, My Good News. She is one who is defeated by memories of the battles of the past. She cannot set herself free. She cannot hear My Voice. She does not understand the Good News of My Love that will redeem the past. *Be* My forgiving Love to her this day. *Be* My hand extended. Let Me touch her through you in mercy.

MONDAY   Psalms 20:6-8; 23:2-3,5

He restores my soul.   Psalm 23:3a

Rest in Me now for your labors have been arduous. Rest beside the still waters. I have brought you through a situation of turmoil, and the storm has now abated. Rest in Me as I set you in green pastures. Let Me anoint your head with the oil of My Joy. Let Me fill you to overflowing with My refreshing Love. Let Me renew your spirit now.

TUESDAY St. Luke 10:2-9; St. Matthew 28:18-20

And lo, I am with you always, to the close of the age. St. Matthew 28:20b

This mission is an important one, although it may not seem so to you. Lift it to Me now. *Release* it to Me—every detail. Know that I will be within you—in the midst of this gathering. I will be present in Love and in Power to teach and to heal and to bless.

WEDNESDAY Philippians 4:6-9,4

Rejoice in the Lord always; again I will say, Rejoice. Philippians 4:4

Many will come seeking My face, but all will not find Me because they come in fear, not in praise. In thanksgiving let your requests be made known to Me. Then My Peace will be the signing that I have begun to work in this situation as you release it completely to Me. *Turn it over to Me.* Take your hands off; your worry-thoughts only hold back the answer. Claim My victory in this matter with praise and thanksgiving. Let Me consecrate your thoughts to see victory before it becomes manifest on the earthly plane. Let Me use your imagination to see this victory as if it had already occurred. It is being formed slowly now.

THURSDAY St. Matthew 21:21-22

And whatever you ask in prayer, you will receive, if you have faith. St. Matthew 21:22

When you hold thoughts of concern about your loved ones, you tear down the work that I am doing in their lives. You hold back the very answer that you seek. Once you have faced their needs firmly and squarely, give them to Me *in expectancy.* I have purposes for their lives that are higher than yours. I can open up a way to help them where there is no way. Trust them to Me. Continue in thanksgiving—regardless of feelings or symptoms.

FRIDAY Psalm 127:1-3

Unless the Lord builds the house, those who build it labor in vain. Unless the Lord watches over the city, the watchman stays awake in vain. Psalm 127:1

Cease your straining. Unless I build this home, your labors will be in vain. Do not think that you created your children: you were only My instrument. They are My gift to you. Do not strive in tensions about things that are not part of My Plan for this home. Let Me build the foundations of the house of Life for your children. You are the watchman, but unless I watch over your home, your staying awake is in vain. I give you sleep, My beloved. Let your work be done creatively in Love, not in anxious toil tomorrow.

SATURDAY   II Corinthians 6:16-7:1

Since we have these promises, beloved, let us cleanse our-selves from every defilement of body and spirit, and make holiness perfect in the fear of God.   II Corinthians 7:1

Beloved, *you* are the temple of My Holy Spirit. Do not willfully defile My temple. You have a very great part to play in the cleansing of the temple, for I will not overrule your free-dom of will. You must make holiness your aim. You must by an act of will cleanse yourself from the habits that defile your body—gluttony is one of them. Do not expose yourself to the old temptations, but replace them with greater love for Me. Take My hand for I am your Father. You cannot do this cleans-ing alone but *I cannot do it without your surrender of will!* You must *want* to be Mine more than to lean on the old crutches, the old defiling habits.

SUNDAY   Hebrews 2:14-15; 4:12-13

For the word of God is living and active, sharper than any two-edged sword, piercing to the division of soul and spirit, of joints and marrow, and discerning the thoughts and intentions of the heart.   Hebrews 4:12

In your work with others do not try to argue: for the enemy loves to create dissension, and he will try to blind their minds with half-truths. Wait in quietness upon Me and let Me speak through you the words that will cut through their secret bondages. Let the Word of God be spoken through your lips. Be the Light to illumine the murky shadows in their hearts. You will be amazed to see their response. I need your voice to proclaim My good news in their special needs. Take none of the glory to yourself.

MONDAY   Psalm 107:33-43

Whoever is wise, let him give heed to these things; let men consider the steadfast love of the Lord.   Psalm 107:43

Your life was once a desert, a wasteland, a bare and un-fruitful field, but I have turned it into an abundantly fertile land. My streams of living waters flow out to those who come thirsting to you; for the blessings you have received from Me are to be shared with the needy. I will bring low the proud and raise up the humble. Those who hunger after My righteousness shall be fed. My steadfast Love enfolds them. I need you to labor in My Love—to sow the fields and plant the vineyards. Be My tiller of the soil today.

TUESDAY   Isaiah 31:1-9

Like birds hovering, so the Lord of hosts will protect Jerusalem; he will protect and deliver it, he will spare and rescue it.   Isaiah 31:5

Do not trust in man-made weapons of destruction but in My Power to deliver your land from the enemy. I will protect My people when they turn back to Me and leave their rebellious ways. Prophesy to the people to destroy their idols, for I am not pleased by their revolt against Me. They have run after false gods of security. They must repent and return to their trust in Me. Then I will move against those who do evil. Those who stumble others will be judged by My judgments.

WEDNESDAY   Isaiah 50:2b; Psalm 34:3-7

I sought the Lord, and he answered me, and delivered me from all my fears.   Psalm 34:4

Look to Me for deliverance from your fears, for My hand is not shortened today. The enemy is tempting the young to lead them astray, but My angels will be watching over those who want to be saved. As I delivered My servant David, so I can deliver your loved one today. Be steadfast in praise. Boast not in the accomplishments of man but in the mercy of God. Sing praises to the Name of the Lord whose mercy endures forever.

THURSDAY   Philippians 2:12-13

For God is at work in you, both to will and to work for his good pleasure.   Philippians 2:13

You are My beloved. When you obey My commands, I am abiding within you to work out the details of your life. You need fear nothing but the loss of Me, for I can bring good out of evil and transform this situation. Turn each decision of your life over to Me so that I can fulfill My destiny for your life. I am working out your salvation but you must surrender your will to Me. Trust only in Me.

FRIDAY   Hebrews 5:14; Romans 12:21

But solid food is for the mature, for those who have their faculties trained by practice to distinguish good from evil. Hebrews 5:14

I have been feeding you solid food so that you might be trained by practice to discern the good from the evil. You are to lead others away from the power of the enemy. By your witness feed them with the solid food. You were once a child feeding only on milk. As you become mature in My Love, I can lead you into deeper understanding of My Word. Feed on My Word: grow strong in My promises. Overcome evil with good.

SATURDAY   Psalm 107:23-32

Let them thank the Lord for his steadfast love, for his wonderful works to the sons of men!   Psalm 107:31

Thanksgiving is the spirit in which sacrifices are to be made—not gloomily out of duty, but joyously! Those who have seen the storm at sea become stilled by My command can rejoice: for they have experienced My steadfast Love in the face of overwhelming difficulties. Faith is not just a feeling. It is *obedience* to My commands to trust in Me. Praise is accepting My blessings by faith even before you see the answer to your prayers.

SUNDAY   St. Luke 9:62; Hebrews 10:36-39

Jesus said to him, "No one who puts his hand to the plow and looks back is fit for the kingdom of God."   St. Luke 9:62

Yes, My child, you will need endurance. Those who are My chosen ones will hold fast in faith no matter how great the testings. If you run away from this crisis, you will be like the man who puts his hand to the plow and then turns back. There can be no turning back for those who are totally committed to Me. For I am coming sooner than you think. Have faith in My Word. Be constant in the face of dangers and troubles. Be centered in Me.

MONDAY   Psalm 107:17-22

Let them thank the Lord for his steadfast love, for his wonderful works to the sons of men!   Psalm 107:21

When My people sin against My Will, they break the laws of health. Sin is voluntary disobedience to My Will. The separation that follows is automatic. You cannot be at one with Me if you are unwilling to accept My Will: for this point of difference will stand between us. When you repent and cry out for My forgiveness, the wall of separation that you have built will come tumbling down. I will set you free from this bondage and save your life from destruction. When you repent for the sin of the world, I will use your prayers for the healing of the nations. Let your witness to Me be made effective in joy.

TUESDAY II Peter 3:17; Hebrews 10:26-31

It is a fearful thing to fall into the hands of the living God. Hebrews 10:31

This one who vexes you is a product of the sin of the world. He has set his will deliberately against Mine. You do not need to be afraid of him for I have overcome the world. Keep the protective circle of purifying fire around you so that nothing of evil may come from him into your spirit to poison you or to harm your body. Beware (when you think you are strong) lest you fall through pride or self-righteousness into the enemy's trap—even as this one has strayed into the devil's clutches. Be wise to protect yourself by claiming My Blood. Let Me stand always between you and him. Leave him to Me. Only My Spirit can save him. Do not resent him or judge him. Judgment is Mine.

WEDNESDAY—Hebrews 10:29-39; Matthew 7:1

But we are not of those who shrink back and are destroyed, but of those who have faith and keep their souls. Hebrews 10:39

Not all will be saved although all have been offered the promise of salvation. Fear not so much for those who have not yet heard the Good News but rather for those who (having heard) have rejected Me. There are many in today's world who have spurned Me after having received the knowledge of My Truth. Pray for endurance and faith that you, too, may not slip back but may keep your souls in the Will of God: in Righteousness and Truth. Judgment is a boomerang that returns upon the one who judges. Pray for those who deny Me. Give them to Me.

THURSDAY   I Corinthians 15:55-58

> *O death, where is thy victory? O death, where is thy sting?*
> I Corinthians 15:55

Have you not fully recognized My victory over death? You prayed earnestly for this person to be healed and much healing of the mind and spirit took place in this life so that she is prepared to enter the Larger Life. She is now healed in My Nearer Presence—but you are still holding on to your desire for physical healing because of your pride. You prayed and things did not happen as you wanted. This is the sting of death. Let Me remove it. Release this person to Me and know that I can bring victory even out of her death. Accept the comfort of My healing Love and Joy in your own heart now.

FRIDAY   II Corinthians 1:3-5

> *For as we share abundantly in Christ's sufferings, so through Christ we share abundantly in comfort too.*
> II Corinthians 1:5

My Peace can comfort you in this time of testing and affliction. My merciful Peace can wash away your remorse over anything you said or thought or did—or failed to do in this relationship. Give Me *all* of your nagging thoughts—your true guilts and the false accusations from the enemy. As you allow My Spirit to comfort you, I can make you able to comfort others. You will find many who will walk the lonely path you are now walking. But you are *not alone* for I am with you! The blessing of My Presence will enable you to help others to find this same blessing in their times of need.

SATURDAY I Corinthians 1:17-25

For the foolishness of God is wiser than men, and the weakness of God is stronger than men. I Corinthians 1:25

You have been depending too much on human eloquence to sway those whom you have tried to help. The wisdom of the world has been made foolish in its inability to solve these desperate problems which threaten to destroy it. To Jews and Gentiles, the crucified Christ has been a stumbling block; but to those who believe and are saved, the Cross has power to overcome. The Father has destroyed the wisdom and cleverness of unbelievers by raising up the weak from their folly through My atoning Love.

SUNDAY I Corinthians 3:18-4:2

So let no one boast of men. For all things are yours, whether Paul or Apollos or Cephas or the world or life or death or the present or the future, all are yours; and you are Christ's; and Christ is God's. I Corinthians 3:21-23

The world's wisdom is futile. To serve the Father is to belong to Him in awareness of His Love and Power. He passes by the wise and gives His gifts to the weak. You are not to boast of men but only to submit yourselves to My Will. You are called to be stewards of the divine mysteries: to be My servants in Love. You are called to be trustworthy in ministering through the Power of My Love.

MONDAY   Hebrews 11:1-3

Now faith is the assurance of things hoped for, the conviction of things not seen.   Hebrews 11:1

Faith endures even when facts contradict. Faith is the inner knowledge of a reality that does not appear outwardly but is received by divine assurance. You cannot comprehend the magnitude of My creation: you can only accept by faith its wonder. For by My Word the things that were not seen were made to appear. By My Word things that are yet only hoped for will become visible. Be the instrument of faith that I can use. Let My Spirit convict you of the reality of things not yet seen. *Believe for others* until they can be believed into believing in Me.

TUESDAY   Ephesians 5:15-20

Therefore do not be foolish, but understand what the will of the Lord is.   Ephesians 5:17

Do not waste time, My children, for it is precious. In these difficult days it is even more important for you to understand and obey My Will. Be filled with My Holy Spirit. Put your dependence on Me—not on eating or drinking or smoking or tranquilizers. These are "escape mechanisms" that only create more problems. The solution to your tensions of the times is deeper commitment of your will to Me. Give Me your problems and give thanks that they are now *Mine*—not yours!

WEDNESDAY   I Corinthians 4:1-5

Therefore do not pronounce judgment before the time, before the Lord comes, who will bring to light the things now hidden in darkness and will disclose the purposes of the heart. Then every man will receive his commendation from God.   I Corinthians 4:5

You are all called to be My trustworthy stewards but some of you have been judging each other. You cannot know the innermost thoughts of another's heart. When I come again, I will expose the secret yearnings and the purposes in their hearts. My judgment is just, but your knowledge is only in part. Judge not—lest you yourself be judged. I will reward the good and the evildoers in My divine justice.

THURSDAY   I John 5:14-15

And this is the confidence which we have in him, that if we ask anything according to his will he hears us.   I John 5:14

You are to ask for much, My child—but in accordance with My Will, for it is higher and better than your will. You ask for baubles, but I want to give you the pearl of great price. When you ask in My Name you are asking in accordance with

My Nature. You may be confident that I hear your requests and that I am answering the prayers that are made in accordance with My Will. I am more willing to give than you are to ask for the fullness of My Will to be done in this situation. Ask in trust—in expectancy—so that you may receive.

FRIDAY   I John 1:5-10

If we confess our sins, he is faithful and just, and will forgive our sins and cleanse us from all unrighteousness.
I John 1:9

Do not be afraid to face this dark area in your life. I want to cleanse and purify you so that you can walk in the Light— not hampered by this darkness of the past. There is one you have not quite forgiven, yet you claim to be without sin. Unforgiveness of others is a sin against Me, for I love this one you will not forgive. Confess to Me your lovelessness. Then I can forgive you and begin to heal this relationship. When you hold jealousy or hurt pride it is *yourself* who is being damaged—not the other person! Confess and accept My forgiveness now.

SATURDAY   Hebrews 10:5-17

I will remember their sins and their misdeeds no more.
Hebrews 10:17

My desire is not for man-made sin offerings of bulls or sheep but for a repentant heart. Can you reply with Me to the Father: "I have come to do Thy Will"? In My earthly Body I took upon Myself your sins. You have been atoned for by My sacrifice. If you will accept this, My gift of freedom from guilt, you will walk out a new person. Stand on My promises that I will no longer remember the sins that you have offered to Me to be nailed to My Cross. *Rejoice and be free!*

SUNDAY   I Corinthians 2:1-10

But, as it is written, "What no eye has seen, nor ear heard, nor the heart of man conceived, what God has prepared for those who love him," God has revealed to us through the Spirit.   I Corinthians 2:9-10a

Do not be afraid, My child, to proclaim the Truth of My resurrected Power. You are not sent by Me to impress men with your words of eloquence or lofty wisdom but only to know Me as your crucified Lord and to demonstrate My Spirit working in Power through your weakness. Your faith is not in man's weakness. Your faith is not in man's wisdom, but in My resurrection Power. The wisdom I will use you to impart is not of man but rather the secret, hidden Truth of the Father's Love. Proclaim this Love that none can fully comprehend except by My Spirit. *Be My Love* ministering to the mature who have worshiped the intellect and failed to see or hear or transmit My all-encompassing Love revealed through My Spirit.

MONDAY   I Corinthians 2:10-13

For the Spirit searches everything, even the depths of God. I Corinthians 2:10b

My Holy Spirit will use your spirit to search the depths of their hearts—not to judge them but to release by faith My

Spirit and My Power in the hidden memories of the past. You are not to be led by the spirit of the world but by My Spirit to help others to understand the God-given supernatural gifts of the Spirit. These are foolishness to those who cannot spiritually discern them. But to those who possess the Spirit of God, they are Light and Wisdom and Power to minister My Love to the world.

TUESDAY   Romans 12:1-2

Do not be conformed to this world but be transformed by the renewal of your mind, that you may prove what is the will of God, what is good and acceptable and perfect. Romans 12:2

The world is seeking to make you conform to its idol worship, its status symbols, its security promises, and its false images. Check your life against the Person I have revealed to you in My earthly ministry. Present yourself daily to Me to be transformed by the making new of your mind, your attitudes, your values. When you are conformed to My Will in your heart, you will get the true guidance you need. You will come to know what is the transformed life.

WEDNESDAY   Acts 2:15-21

And it shall be that whoever calls on the name of the Lord shall be saved.   Acts 2:21

Are you ready? Heed the warnings of My prophet Joel and prophesy. For My Spirit is being outpoured upon young men who are seeing visions and old men who are dreaming dreams. Young and old are receiving the fullness of My Spirit that they may be empowered to endure in the difficult days ahead. My Joy will be their strength and they shall call upon My Name and they shall be saved.

THURSDAY   Acts 2:37-42

And Peter said to them, "Repent, and be baptized every one of you in the name of Jesus Christ for the forgiveness of your sins; and you shall receive the gift of the Holy Spirit.   Acts 2:38

After repentance, you can accept the forgiveness of sins that was made available for you on the Cross. My Holy Spirit falls upon converted flesh—those who have accepted My forgiveness. The promise is to all—not to any one particular color or creed or age-group. This is a crooked generation running in rebellion against Me after forbidden fruit and false gods. Those who receive My Holy Spirit will devote themselves to the study of My Word, to fellowship with Me and others of My children. Give time for prayer. Receive Me in the breaking of bread as I commanded you on the night I was betrayed. *Be* My temple.

FRIDAY   St. John 14:25-26; St. Matthew 9:17

But the Counselor, the Holy Spirit, whom the Father will send in my name, he will teach you all things, and bring to your remembrance all that I have said to you.   St. John 14:26

I have bestowed upon you My Holy Spirit, the Counselor, whom the Father has sent to guide you. You must leave off your old ways and be guided into My deeper Truth. Do not try to put this new wine into old wineskins, old thought patterns and values and habits. Be eager to be changed as I recall to your mind the areas in your life that need to be conformed to My will. I will remind you. Are you willing to *let go of this old habit?*

SATURDAY St. Matthew 7:13-27

For the gate is narrow and the way is hard, that leads to life, and those who find it are few. St. Matthew 7:14

You are feeling divided, frustrated, and confused because you have let too many human voices distract you from keeping your eyes on My Will for your life. Surrender all of these needs to Me. I know them far better than you do. I can sort them out and give you the right priorities. Build your house upon My Rock. Do only those things that are My highest Will. You may be tempted to do many good things that will distract you from the best. Seek My guidance *now* about all these matters.

SUNDAY St. John 15:16-17

You did not choose me, but I chose you and appointed you that you should go and bear fruit and that your fruit should abide; so that whatever you ask the Father in my name, he may give it to you. St. John 15:16

You are to bear much fruit—fruit that will endure and not perish. When you are used by Me to help others, do not take the glory to yourself or the fruit will be tainted. Do not let others put you on the throne of their hearts else you will sin by usurping My place. When you must refuse to see them, do so in prayer that I will touch them through your love. I can send another of My helpers if now you cannot meet their needs. Pray each time the telephone rings—for My Wisdom. Then do whatever I give you to do in My Joy. Leave their needs in My hands. In Love, lift them after each meeting and *release them to Me*.

MONDAY I John 4:16-21

> *So we know and believe the love God has for us. God is love, and he who abides in love abides in God, and God abides in him.* I John 4:16

This one is being healed by My Love poured through you. When you feel impatient, ask Me for more of My Love in you. Take your eyes off the person and *fix them on Me*. Satan is attacking you and him with doubt and fear. You can claim the Power of My Blood over this situation now. Command this spirit of fear to get out of you in the Name of Jesus Christ. Claim My Love now to fill the pockets vacated by the enemy. Put a circle of My purifying fire around you for protection. Now lift the person to Me again and let My Love saturate him, filling every cell of his body. Think of him as immersed in My Love now.

TUESDAY St. Luke 15:3-7; II Corinthians 3:4-6

> *Just so, I tell you, there will be more joy in heaven over one sinner who repents than over ninety-nine righteous persons who need no repentance.* St. Luke 15:7

This day you will know that I came to save the lost sheep. Let Me make a pathway to this one who needs to be loved. Let

Me open a door in her heart. She is straying because of past circumstances that have made her a victim of the sins of others. Be patient in My Patience. Be loving in My Love. Your human love will not be sufficient but your sufficiency is of God who has called you to be a minister of reconciliation to her.

WEDNESDAY   St. Luke 14:16-24

And the master said to the servant, "Go out to the highways and hedges, and compel people to come in, that my house may be filled."   St. Luke 14:23

I have prepared for you a feast, but you are denying My invitation. You are making excuses, but they are not valid reasons. Why are you afraid of committing more of your life to Me? If you reject this call to a deeper walk with Me you will be left outside like those in the parable when the doors to the banquet hall were closed. I will bring in the poor and the lame and the blind to fill the seats that have been rejected by the invited guests.

THURSDAY   James 5:13-16; I Corinthians 12:14-27

Now you are the body of Christ and individually members of it.   I Corinthians 12:27

Share your difficulties with one another in your prayer group. Pray for one another. Shared burdens become lighter. There is a need for fellowship where the group can be refueled by My fire. I will be there in the midst of you. I created you for fellowship with Me and with each other. Let your prayer-group meetings be the joyous lifting of your problems to Me. Often it takes more than one to lift the heavier loads. Beware lest you all wallow together in the problems. Lift them and *leave them to Me.* Then rejoice as you go your separate ways. Continue to claim the victories in thanksgiving.

FRIDAY I Thessalonians 5:16-22

Rejoice always. I Thessalonians 5:16

Anyone can rejoice when the pathway of life is smooth! Anyone can give thanks in time of victory. Most men pray in times of real trouble. But I ask you, My disciple, to pray *constantly*—without ceasing—in My Spirit. Do not quench My Spirit with your doubts and self-pity, but rejoice in *all* circumstances, even those that seem to you to be evil, for I can bring good out of them. Abstain from evil yourself as you test the spirits. Heed My prophecies for they are given to warn you, to exhort you, to comfort you. My Will is for you to *give thanks at all times!*

SATURDAY II Thessalonians 3:1-3; St. Matthew 6:13

But the Lord is faithful; he will strengthen you and guard you from evil. II Thessalonians 3:3

There are those who are jealous of you as men were jealous of Me in My earthly ministry. Satan loves to use jealousy to attack My servants. You must hold on to Me in faith and I will be faithful to you. I will protect you. I will keep you from harm and give you My Love and strength to comfort you when others condemn you falsely. Be not afraid of what others may say or do. You are responsible to Me. Seek only My direction. In love, be steadfast—no matter what others may say.

SUNDAY   Ephesians 5:14-6:4

For the husband is the head of the wife as Christ is the head of the church, his body, and is himself its Savior. Ephesians 5:23

Because of the deterioration of home life in today's world you find yourselves beset by a multitude of problems. It is because home relationships have been distorted. When you, my son, abdicated your rightful place as spiritual head of your home, you left "the job of religion" to your wife. When you worshiped the gods of money and power (so that you were too busy to be a husband to your wife and a father to your children) you abdicated your rightful place. Material things are no substitute for real love. Children starve in loveless opulence. Wives become neurotic escapists when their husbands give only material possessions but fail to give love and spiritual strength to the home. Nagging ruins any relationship—praying restores it. Turn back, O man, before it is too late. Let Me *be* Head in you. Let Me transform your home!

MONDAY   I Corinthians 11:3

But I want you to understand that the head of every man is Christ, the head of a woman is her husband, and the head of Christ is God.   I Corinthians 11:3

If in every home the man would make Me Lord of his life and take his rightful place as head of his household, there would be less confusion in the world. The wife who is submissive to her husband (who is submissive to Me) has the joy of fulfilling her commitment to Me in her role of comforting and sustaining her mate. But when the husband denies Me, she is torn between her personal commitment to Me and her marriage vow to him. Pray for all men that they may become the spiritual heads of their homes. In turning religious responsibilities over to their wives, My sons have abdicated from the very purpose for which they were created: to be the spiritual heads of their homes as I am Head in them!

TUESDAY   Ephesians 5:21-33

Be subject to one another out of reverence for Christ.
Ephesians 5:21

When husband and wife are *both* subject to Me, they can form the relationship in marriage that is holy love—like that between Me and My Church. When the husband loves his wife as I love the Church, he loves her enough to give up his self-will for her good: as I gave up My life for the sanctification of My Body the Church. He loves her as I love—to cherish her, *not to crush her!* When a husband lets his mother or father dominate him and separate him from his wife, he is failing in My divine ordinance: that the man is to leave father and mother and cleave to his wife so that the two may be joined as one. Make love your aim to *complete* each other.

WEDNESDAY   Ephesians 5:33-6:4

Fathers, do not provoke your children to anger, but bring them up in the discipline and instruction of the Lord.
Ephesians 6:4

Too many homes are battlegrounds. They are not centers of My healing Love where the members can be refreshed after the day's struggles are over. My Will is for the wife to respect her husband and care for *his* needs (as well as those of the children). The husband is to *love* his wife—as fully as he loves himself! If each one of you truly prefers the other in love, there will be harmony in the home where children can learn obedience and be instructed and disciplined as needed—but in *love*, not in anger. You (who are parents) remember not to provoke anger in your children. Not all teasing is funny. Avoid the tense conflicts of will in the home by praying together for My Will to be done in *each* of you. A family can be a prayer cell or group, not a battleground.

THURSDAY   Psalm 116:16-19; Isaiah 6:8

And I heard the voice of the Lord saying, "Whom shall I send, and who will go for us?" Then I said, "Here am I! Send me."   Isaiah 6:8

The sacrifice of thanksgiving gladdens My heart. When you come into My Presence, let it be in a spirit of praise. When you make your fresh vow of commitment to Me each morning, let it be in a spirit of praise and thanksgiving—not in heaviness, as if it were a burdensome duty to offer your life afresh to Me. Let it be in the spirit of My servant Isaiah: "Here am I, Lord. Send Me." Let Me touch your lips afresh each morning with a burning coal. Let Me anoint you each day with My Spirit of gladness.

FRIDAY   Ephesians 5:15-17; II Peter 2:1-10

But false prophets also arose among the people, just as there will be false teachers among you, who will secretly bring in destructive heresies, even denying the Master who bought them, bringing upon themselves swift destruction. II Peter 2:1

Yes, there are many evils besetting the world, for the devil is trying to make the most of his remaining time. He is deceiving even leaders in the Church with his subtle heresies so that man tries to usurp the prerogatives of God. He is dividing husbands and wives, children and parents. The lawlessness of Satan is being evidenced in every area of life. It behooves you, My sons and daughters, to walk more carefully. Pray to be shown how to use your time wisely. Pray to be in My *highest* Will at all times. The good is not enough: it must be the *best* use of your talents, resources, and time in these difficult last days.

SATURDAY   I Peter 4:7-11

As each has received a gift, employ it for one another, as good stewards of God's varied grace.   I Peter 4:10

You are called to be a wise steward of My grace. I give you My Strength, My Wisdom, My Power to live each day. Do everything to the glory of the Father who has dominion over all things. *Use* the gifts I have given you: not just the natural gifts but the supernatural ones as well. Walk in the spirit of Wisdom so that your life blesses others. Do not be afraid to share your gifts with others. They are given you in trust. They are meant *to be used to My glory!*

SUNDAY   Ephesians 5:18-20

Always and for everything giving thanks in the name of our Lord Jesus Christ to God the Father.   Ephesians 5:20

When you are truly filled with My Spirit, you do not need other spirits to give you a lift. I am concerned about those who claim that their bodies are the temples of My Holy Spirit—yet they express their insecurity by dependencies on alcoholic spirits, nicotinic spirits and gluttonous spirits. When a heart is filled with gratitude for the wonders of My Forgiveness and Love, there is no craving for these material escape mechanisms. Fill your minds, My children, with Scriptures and hymns so that your life will be lived each day against the background music of praise and thanksgiving.

MONDAY   I Peter 4:12-16

But rejoice in so far as you share Christ's sufferings, that you may also rejoice and be glad when his glory is revealed.   I Peter 4:13

Suffering has come upon you, My child, but it is only to prove your faith in Me. Hold fast to My Truth and you shall not be dismayed when others desert you or reproach you for My sake. Remain steadfast in prayer and I shall overcome this evil assault of the enemy. Continue to glorify Me in praise and I shall restore this situation. My Power shall be resting upon you when it is needed. Go in faith, nothing doubting, when I call you to go in My Name. Fear not the interference of the enemy. I shall vindicate My Plan. I shall be glorified in this problem.

TUESDAY I Peter 4:17-5:5

Tend the flock of God that is your charge, not by con-
straint but willingly, not for shameful gain but eagerly,
not as domineering over those in your charge but being
examples to the flock. I Peter 5:2-3

You are a part of the household of God. You can wonder
about the lot of those who rebel against Me. But do not turn
away from Me because of sufferings. Remain faithful to the
trust I have given *you*—not for personal gain or honor or
out of a sense of duty but in joyous expectancy. Do not dominate those I send to you but lead them: in wisdom reveal to
them the glory that is to come to all of you who remain faithful to Me. Behold, there is tribulation now and·it will increase
until I am manifested to the faithful.

WEDNESDAY Psalm 119:9-16

With my whole heart I seek thee; let me not wander from
thy commandments! Psalm 119:10

My son, seek Me with your whole heart in these hazard-
ous times when many are falling away from My commandments. Meditate on My Word that you may not stray out of
ignorance into ways that are not My ways. Hold to the pure
and fill your mind with the good lest you fall prey to the
enemy. Bear witness to others, exhort them to follow in My
paths. Walk in My Light all the days of your life. There are
many who need to see My Joy revealed in you—to experience
My Power poured out upon this need *through* your ministry
of compassion.

THURSDAY   II Chronicles 7:14

If my people who are called by my name humble themselves, and pray and seek my face, and turn from their wicked ways, then I will hear from heaven, and will forgive their sin and heal their land.   II Chronicles 7:14

There are many today who have not sought My face in prayer for this nation. They are following the wicked ways of idolatry and sorcery and rebellion and perversion. They have shut their ears to My Voice and their eyes no longer seek the Truth of My Word. They are called by My Name but they no longer believe in the Power of My Name. They no longer pray in humility although My people are perishing in sin that cannot be turned back except by prayer. Call together the elders for a fast. Repent of these sins that I may be able to forgive their sin and heal this land.

FRIDAY   Ephesians 1:17-23

And he has put all things under his feet and has made him the head over all things for the church.   Ephesians 1:22

When I reveal My Wisdom to you, do not be afraid to trust Me to bring to pass the things that I show you. You are a child of the King, an inheritor of the Kingdom of heaven. My Power is immeasurable for I have been given authority and dominion over everything, not only now but forever. My desire is to build up My Church in fullness, to give enlightenment and grace to those who respond to My call. Today, Beloved, *live* in this revelation. Let Me enlighten you to see that you are to pray with My authority over the enemy.

Take dominion in My Name over the evil that is hampering your life.

SATURDAY   Isaiah 58:6-12

Then you shall call, and the Lord will answer; you shall cry, and he will say, Here I am.   Isaiah 58:9a

By prayer and fasting this one shall be delivered. I choose to break the yoke and loose the bonds of the oppressed but *you are needed to pray* the prayer of faith and give comfort to this needy one. My healing Power shall bring new life to My children. Your call shall be answered and I shall be with you in My righteousness. I shall go before you and My Light shall overcome the darkness in the lives of the afflicted. If you pour yourself out for the weak and let Me use you to feed the hungry, you shall be like a watered garden. The springs of My Love will never fail you but will flow out continuously.

SUNDAY   Joel 1:14-2:28

You shall know that I am in the midst of Israel, and that I, the Lord, am your God and there is none else. And my people shall never again be put to shame.   Joel 2:27

Call the people to repentance, for I am not pleased with their disrespect of Me and their rebellion against My commandments. They have brought punishment upon themselves. The day of the Lord is approaching and many will cry out in anger and despair as their idols are destroyed by fire. A great people shall be in anguish, and a land like Eden shall be turned to a wilderness unless My people repent of their evil and return to their God. You are to rend your hearts and fast and pray for My mercy to spare this stiff-necked people. You have received the early rain. I will send the latter rain and restore the years that the locusts have eaten.

MONDAY   Malachi 3:13-4:3

But for you who fear my name the sun of righteousness shall rise, with healing in its wings.   Malachi 4:2a

The day of reckoning will come upon the evildoers; the proud and the rebellious will be brought low. The chaff will be burned and their wickedness will not be allowed to escape notice. I shall distinguish between the righteous who serve Me and the wicked who flaunt My Will. In the book of remembrance there is a record of those who have been faithful to Me. They shall see the sun of righteousness arise. There shall be healing for those who love Me and keep My commandments.

TUESDAY   Ephesians 4:1-3

I therefore, a prisoner for the Lord, beg you to lead a life worthy of the calling to which you have been called. Ephesians 4:1

My child, I have called you but *your response* to My call makes the difference in your life. If you respond in humility and with patience, I can use you to help maintain the unity of the Spirit in this time of stress. If you continue to forgive those who cannot hear or accept what I am saying through you, My witness of Love can maintain peace. If you become discouraged or impatient or arrogant with them, you will not be leading a life worthy of your calling. Keep your eyes fixed on Me and pray in love for *all:* that My Spirit will guide them and deliver them from deceit that the enemy has planted in them.

WEDNESDAY   Acts 4:31; 16:25-26

And they were all filled with the Holy Spirit and spoke the word of God with boldness.   Acts 4:31b

When My apostles prayed, the power released was great enough to shake the places where they prayed. They were enabled to speak My Truth with boldness and even the doors of a prison were shaken open. Are you, My children, praying with that kind of faith in this situation where the enemy has attacked? Satan has tried to divide the flock but I can use you as prayer warriors to release My Power so that he will not be able to cripple and scatter the faithful. *Claim dominion over his deceits;* remain constant in prayer in your groups until the enemy yields to the Power of My Holy Spirit.

THURSDAY   St. Matthew 18:19-20; James 4:7

Again I say to you, if two of you agree on earth about anything they ask, it will be done for them by my Father in heaven.   St. Matthew 18:19

My children, I have told you to ask in My Name as you gather together. Ask whatever is *in My Nature to give:* for I shall be there in your midst to answer. It is My Will to protect My work. Ask, claiming dominion over the evil forces that hamper My children's growth in the Spirit. *Believe* that

I broke Satan's power on Calvary. Claim that victory in this present dissension in your prayer group or cell, in your Church, in your home. Do not let the devil divide and scatter. Pray for more love for each other, but bind the evil one. *Resist* the enemy and he will flee from your work.

FRIDAY   Psalm 86

I give thanks to thee, O Lord my God, with my whole heart, and I will glorify thy name for ever.   Psalm 86:12

You have prayed for Me to save your life, your ministry, your family well-being. Now *claim* My victory. *Know* that I answer you. Like David, when you pray, accept the reality of My Love for you. Spread your needs before Me—like a child coming to the earthly father. How much *more* can you depend on Me, My children, to save and protect you in these difficult times! Call upon Me in the time of trouble—but then take your eyes off the problems and *claim My victory in praise!* Give thanks. Accept the victory in advance. What is now claimed in the spiritual victory will become manifested on the earthly plane.

SATURDAY   Isaiah 12:1-6

Shout, and sing for joy, O inhabitant of Zion, for great in your midst is the Holy One of Israel.   Isaiah 12:6

Yea, I am the God of your salvation and with joy you will draw water from the wells. You will call upon My Name in praise and thanksgiving for I have forgiven your sin. You will prophesy to My glory among the nations; and wherever I call you to follow Me, you will go in My Strength and My

Joy. You will trust and not fear what man can say or do. You have humbled yourself before Me and I shall comfort you. Go in peace.

SUNDAY   Psalm 37:1-3

Trust in the Lord, and do good; so you will dwell in the land, and enjoy security.   Psalm 37:3

Now that you have prayed deeply about this problem, leave it in My hands. Do not fret about those who deny Me. Do not be envious of those who enjoy the idolatry of others. Do not be impatient—for justice is Mine. Your responsibility is to do only what *I* command you to do in this situation. Trust in Me. Do what I have given *you* to do. Take delight in whatever I have given you to do—no matter how small or insignificant the task. I will give you the deep desire of your heart to walk in union with Me. Stay committed to Me in *all* areas of your life. I will act. *Trust in Me.*

MONDAY   Revelation 22:14-15; Isaiah 8:19-22

Blessed are those who wash their robes, that they may have the right to the tree of life and that they may enter the city by the gates.   Revelation 22:14

On My return many of you will be counted among those who have washed their robes in the Blood of the Lamb— those who have joyfully and earnestly accepted the cleansing power of My Blood to redeem your past sins and heal your brokenness. You shall enter into the holy city and live eternally. But there are many today who flaunt their wickedness: the sorcerers who ignore the commandments of My Word and who conjure up magic; who commune with demonic spirits preying upon the weak and ignorant and confused; those who claim to be contacting the dead when they are opening themselves to Satan. They (like murderers, idolaters, and fornicators) shall be left outside the city gates—unless they repent.

TUESDAY   Revelation 21:8; I Samuel 15:23

But as for the cowardly, the faithless, the polluted, as for murderers, fornicators, sorcerers, idolaters, and all liars, their lot shall be in the lake that burns with fire and brimstone, which is the second death.   Revelation 21:8

Beware of those who tell you to defy My Word because it is obsolete. Do not traffic with those who tell you that they can give you power over other people, sexual and material power or power to shape the future to suit their own wills. Beware of mediums and seances and prophetesses of the occult for they are dealing with lying, seducing spirits—*not* the *Holy Spirit* of God! Shun them: else you bring upon yourself the fate of Saul who disobeyed Me in consulting the witch of Endor. They are like murderers and liars and idolaters in that they rebel against My commandments. They shall be held accountable on the Day of Judgment. The second death shall be the result of their sinfulness if they do not repent of their sins and believe in Me.

WEDNESDAY   Revelation 21:1-4; St. Matthew 25:1-13

Behold the dwelling of God is with men. He will dwell with them, and they shall be his people, and God himself will be with them.   Revelation 21:3b

Beloved, the time will come when every tear will be wiped away and there shall be no pain and no grieving and

no death—only life eternal for those who have chosen to dwe¹¹
with Me. Old things will have passed away and there will be
a new creation. Faint not during these times of tribulation but
hold fast to your faith in God. You are My people for you
obey My commands and I shall come in time to set you free.
Only be patient and faithful, persevering in righteousness,
ready like the bridesmaids with your wicks trimmed and your
lamps filled with oil.

THURSDAY   Revelation 21:5-6; Acts 16:31

*And he who sat upon the throne said, "Behold, I make
all things new."*   Revelation 21:5a

My promise is to you who hold fast, who win out over
temptations of doubt and fear. As you keep Me on the throne
of your lives, you will be given water from the fountain of
life. Your thirst will be freely quenched for My Spirit will
abide in your spirit. I am the beginning and the end—trust in
Me, believe *in* Me, and you shall be saved.

FRIDAY   Revelation 21:27; 22:1-5

*And night shall be no more; they need no light of lamp
or sun, for the Lord God will be their light, and they
shall reign for ever and ever.*   Revelation 22:5

The temple of the city of God will be the Lord God
Himself and the Lamb. There will be no place for the deceivers and those who reject Me and practice evil—for their
names will not be recorded in the Book of Life. Those who

have obeyed my commandments and remained faithful to Me will rejoice for they will see God's face and His Name will be on their foreheads. There shall be no more night. The river of the water of life will flow from the throne and the tree of life shall be for the healing of the nations. And the whole company will be crying out in joy: "Hallelujah! For the Lord God Almighty reigns forever."

SATURDAY St. Luke 6:46-49; Jude 17-25

But you, beloved, build yourselves up on your most holy faith; pray in the Holy Spirit. Jude 20

My children, fear not those who scoff and follow their lustful passions. Let your house of Life be built on the firm foundation of obedience to My Truth—not on shifting sands of worldly idols and whims. Walk in My Love and witness to those who doubt so that they may be saved from falling. Pray in My Spirit to be kept from falling yourself. Lest you become proud, rejoice in *My* authority, not your own. I, the Lord, have dominion—now and forever.

SUNDAY Psalm 96

Declare his glory among the nations, his marvelous works among all the peoples! Psalm 96:3

Tell it to the nations, My children, for the Lord is great and His mercy shall be unto all who trust in Me. Sing praises, for the Lord your God reigns—no matter how great your present darkness may seem to you now. Let there be joy in all the earth, for the peoples will be judged with mercy and truth and righteousness. Great is the Father, the Creator. Worship Him who has made heaven and earth. Sing a new song today—a song of honor and praise!

MONDAY Psalm 121

The Lord will keep your going out and your coming in from this time forth and for evermore. Psalm 121:8

Lift up your hearts, your eyes, your voices. For your Lord protects and guides your comings and goings more than you realize. *Know* the Source of your help today. Know that I will protect you in all times of danger or temptation by day or by night. While you sleep, I will watch over you and your loved ones whom you commit to Me. Rest in Me. Trust in Me.

TUESDAY Psalm 146

I will praise the Lord as long as I live; I will sing praises to my God while I have being. Psalm 146:2

Praise, praise, praise—all the day long, My children. I do not need your praise: it is *you* who need to count your blessings and rejoice! I am setting free those who are in prison to their sins and lifting up those who are burdened today. I am giving sight to the blind and strengthening the widows and orphans. Are you a part of the answer to this world's problems? Are you claiming these victories with Me in joyous praise? Or have you let the enemy blind you with self-pity? Have you slipped back into old thought-patterns? Praise changes *your* attitudes, not Mine—for My Love is *constantly* outpoured!

WEDNESDAY   Psalm 144:1-11

Stretch forth thy hand from on high, rescue me and deliver me from the many waters, from the hand of aliens. Psalm 144:7

Your days are limited—no man knows when his time will come—and it is right that you should make the most of them. But you need not strain, My child. Sufficient to each day is the strength and wisdom that I give you. I am concerned about *every detail* of your life. I can stretch out My hand to deliver you from dangerous waters or cruel people, from persecution or lies. I am mindful of your needs. I am your Rock and your Deliverer.

THURSDAY   Romans 8:35-39

For I am sure that neither death, nor life, nor angels, nor principalities, nor things present, nor things to come, nor powers, nor height, nor depth, nor anything else in all creation, will be able to separate us from the love of God in Christ Jesus our Lord.   Romans 8:38-39

When you are praying for someone in grief, be a channel for My comfort to reach her. Lift her up in praise for My Love to touch her—to draw her closer to Myself through this need. Nothing can separate her from My Love, but she does not know this yet. *Be* My Love to her in this time of testing.

Go quietly in My Joy and her spirits will be lifted too. Do not imagine that your prayers were wasted for her loved one: they were used to make easier his transition into the Larger Life.

FRIDAY   Romans 8:28-30

We know that in everything God works for good with those who love him, who are called according to his purpose.   Romans 8:28

Nothing is ever wasted in My service. Through this suffering together a new beauty came into their love for each other. In My Kingdom, he will continue to grow more than he had for many years on earth. You prayed for wholeness. Give thanks that he has been made *whole* in My Nearer Presence—for his mind and spirit and relationships were healed in this earthly life and now his healing is complete in glory. There are no cripples, no cancer-sufferers in Paradise.

SATURDAY—Romans 8:26-27

Likewise the Spirit helps us in our weakness; for we do not know how to pray as we ought, but the Spirit himself intercedes for us with sighs too deep for words.   Romans 8:26

Often you do not know how to pray. In a case like this My Spirit will intercede through you—with words you do not fully understand. My Wisdom is higher than yours, for My Spirit knows the hearts of men and intercedes according to the Will of the Father. When your intellect prays, you are too often hearing your own will or that of others. Listen! In quiet centering in Me, you will hear My Voice speaking through you.

SUNDAY I Peter 4:12-13

But rejoice in so far as you share Christ's sufferings, that you may also rejoice and be glad when his glory is revealed. I Peter 4:13

My people are suffering in parts of the world that are undergoing persecution. Let your shock and grief for them be a crying out to Me that they may be delivered. Lift them daily in prayer: that their faith may be strengthened and their courage endure so that they will not falter. When you think that your own load is heavy, think of those who go hungry and cold for their faith. Then in thanksgiving for your blessings, lift these saints to Me. They are praying for you. Join them in the worldwide fellowship of prayer. Claim with them and for them the glory that will be revealed! I will be able to meet their needs through your prayers.

MONDAY Romans 12:9-12; I John 4:7-21

And this commandment we have from him, that he who loves God should love his brother also. I John 4:21

Loving others is not always easy for you. You must love the sinner even though you may hate the sin. You cannot condone the sin, but you can pray for My Love to save the person from this sin. In Love, claim the Power of My Blood and cut the bondage between this person and the one who leads him astray. In faith, bind the oppressing spirit that causes him to stumble—fear, anxiety, anger, deceit, bitterness, lust, rebellion, or whatever I show you through discernment. Pray for My Love to flood him—a tidal wave of My Love to cleanse him. Pray for My Peace and Joy to fill the emptied areas in his life.

TUESDAY   Romans 12:14-21

Bless those who persecute you; bless and do not curse them.   Romans 12:14

When you do not have enough love to pray thus, you must first come to Me humbly—confessing your *own* sin. To sin is human; but to love and forgive the sinner is divine. It is only My Perfect Love that can cast out the evil spirits oppressing the sinner—not your human love. Confess to Me your spirit of judgment. Ask My forgiveness for *all* your own sins before you ask Me to give you the Power to come against Satan and win victory in this situation. Then pray in My Love. Pray in faith that I will do a *mighty* work in him!

WEDNESDAY   I Corinthians 13:1-8a; Philippians 4:8

Love bears all things, believes all things, hopes all things, endures all things.   I Corinthians 13:7

Love bears all things—it suffers long and is patient. Do not forget how long I have been patient with you, My child. Believe the best for this person. Do not bind him to his past sin. Often the family of the alcoholic holds back the healing. Be firm with him. Hold him up to the *best* that is in him—in faith that I will redeem the past evil (or weakness) and set him free from this miserable bondage. Now hold a new picture of him—see him as the "new person" he *is* becoming. Consecrate your own thoughts: let Me give you a new picture to hold of him until he *becomes* that picture!

THURSDAY St. Matthew 6:34-7:5; Philippians 4:6-9

> *Have no anxiety about anything, but in everything by prayer and supplication with thanksgiving let your requests be made known to God.* Philippians 4:6

Do not let the old anxieties seep back into your mind concerning this person. If you have a "relapse of anxiety," it is just as sinful as for him to slip back into his sin! Your anxiety is a sin, because I have told you not to be anxious; and because it cuts off this person from the lifeline of faith and love which he needs you to channel into him. If you are channeling anxiety, fear, and condemnation, you are holding back his healing. Pray in thanksgiving—*regardless* of your feelings. Pray as an act of *obedience to Me*—not because you feel like it!

FRIDAY I Peter 5:1-6; I Samuel 15:23

> *Clothe yourselves, all of you, with humility toward one another, for "God opposes the proud, but gives grace to the humble."* I Peter 5:5b

The devil would tempt you to resent the authority of the elders. You who are younger can learn from them in humility so that you will not have to make the same mistakes they did. Be not proud and rebellious, for rebellion is as the sin of witchcraft. Be willing to profit from the examples of others whose fruit are manifested—not idolizing them but looking to Me even as My "under-shepherds" do, for I am the Good Shepherd. If you are clothed in humility now, you will be clothed with Me in glory later.

SATURDAY   I Peter 4:1-5

They are surprised that you do not now join them in the same wild profligacy, and they abuse you; but they will give account to him who is ready to judge the living and the dead.   I Peter 4:4-5

There is a true value that comes from physical suffering, although many have distorted this Scripture and are afraid to pray for healing. When you suffered physically from the effects of your own sin and wrong-thinking, you took steps in your life by My Grace to cease from these sins. Part of your physical healing was to change the causes (spiritual and physical). Your spiritual healing was to *want* to live, not by man's passions but by My Will. Some of your friends are surprised—perhaps even taunting you—because you no longer accept the old immoral way of life. That time is past for you because you look to Me for My indwelling Spirit to bring forth "New Life" in you. They will later have to give account to Me for the misuse of My gift of life.

SUNDAY   I Peter 4:7-11

As each has received a gift, employ it for one another, as good stewards of God's varied grace.   I Peter 4:10

My children, you are to be wise stewards of My good gifts to you—not just the gifts of money, time, natural talents, or circumstances in life. You are to glorify Me in the use of the supernatural gifts also. When you speak or minister to the needs of another, do it in My Name. Let Me supply the strength. Do all that you are led by My Spirit to undertake— but do it in humility, not claiming the glory for yourself. Do it in love for each other. These difficult days behoove you to remain wise and constant in prayer. Your hospitality may be the cup of coffee or tea given to a distraught neighbor. Do all to glorify God.

MONDAY   St. Matthew 25:13-30

His master said to him, "Well done, good and faithful servant; you have been faithful over a little, I will set you over much; enter into the joy of your master."   St. Matthew 25:23

You have all been given natural talents—some more than others. It is not the number of talents that is important, but the way in which they are used. Some who have the most talents are distracted and fail to use them wisely. They run from one interest to another and dissipate their energies. But others are too fearful to *use* their talents. They bury them—as if to hoard a treasure. They are afraid to share with others. They waste what has been given freely to them—and, ultimately, what they have is then taken away! Be mindful that you do not in these crucial days waste your talents. To those who use what they have, more will be given.

TUESDAY   St. Matthew 26:6-13

For you always have the poor with you, but you will not always have me.   St. Matthew 26:11

The woman who anointed My head with expensive ointment was not wasting a precious substance—she was giving of her greatest treasure in worship. She was preparing My body symbolically for burial, and she was harshly judged because she did not sell the precious ointment and give the money to the poor. Your "anointing" of one of My little ones may be a part of your worship of Me. You may even feel wasted in a small ministry of prayer when you feel capable of a greater one. When you pray for these My little ones, remember that your precious time and your comforting love are being given to them in worship of Me. I use your life as a precious ointment to anoint them.

WEDNESDAY   St. Matthew 25:31-46

And the King will answer them, "Truly, I say to you, as you did it to one of the least of these my brethren, you did it to me."   St. Matthew 25:40

Many will call upon My Name when I come again on the great white throne of glory. They who have denied Me will be convicted and go away to eternal punishment for their failure to minister to Me through ministering to My little ones in distress. They have denied Me in failing to respond to the needs of the hungry, the naked, the sick and the strangers. All of My people will be judged—the nations will be judged —and the King will answer: "As you did it not to my little ones, you did it not to Me." Now is the time to bring My people to repentance before it is too late. Now is the time for earnest prayer and fasting that your nation may be saved.

THURSDAY   St. Luke 16:10-13

He who is faithful in a very little is faithful also in much; and he who is dishonest in a very little is dishonest also in much.   St. Luke 16:10

Do not fret because you are sometimes feeling torn by the contrasting pulls of life. You cannot serve God and man. Do not be surprised that some who have been dishonest in small ways become major deceivers. Prove yourself to be faithful to Me in little relationships, in little decisions, in the use of whatever gifts you have received. Then you will find it easier to remain faithful as more is given to you. Make My priorities your own. When you feel tense and "pulled apart," it is because you are trying to serve too many masters. Keep Me on the throne of your heart and you will be more loving, more wise in guidance, more usable.

FRIDAY   St. Mark 10:35-40; Romans 12:3

For by the grace given to me I bid every one among you not to think of himself more highly than he ought to think, but to think with sober judgment, each according to the measure of faith which God has assigned him.   Romans 12:3

Are you able to drink of My cup of persecution? Are you willing to be faithful to Me when the way is rough and dangerous? You are so eager to venture into deeper responsibilities of ministry—rather like children who want to help with household chores when it is all new but who tire easily as soon as the newness wears off! My cup will have bitter dregs, and you will be slandered by the jealous and belittled by those who cannot possibly understand. Do not be presumptuous like My servants James and John when they asked for the highest seats. Be willing to take the low seats. Then you may be asked to come up higher.

SATURDAY   St. Mark 10:42-45

For the Son of man also came not to be served but to serve, and to give his life as a ransom for many.   St. Mark 10:45

Are you willing to be a servant to many? Are you willing to wash their feet—even as I washed the feet of My disciples? In the worldly life, those who are great in authority tend to lord it over the less influential or less well educated or less well-reared. The rich or upper class tend to look down upon the poor or lower-class citizens. But in the kingdom of heaven it shall not be so. Whoever claims to be first will become last. Those who would become great must become the servants of all. I have come as one who serves, one who dies for you, My children. Likewise, give your lives for the many whom I will send to you.

SUNDAY   St. Mark 12:13-17

Jesus said to them, "Render to Caesar the things that are Caesar's, and to God the things that are God's." And they were amazed at him.   St. Mark 12:17

When you are confused about your loyalties and responsibilities, do not seek the counsel of men who may only confuse you all the more unless they, too, have had this testing. Ask for the guidance of My Holy Spirit. Look to My words in Scripture. I have already told you to render to Caesar the things that are Caesar's. You must live *in both worlds*. Be a nun or a priest *in the world*. Live within this world's confines, but *not of this world!* Accept the laws of your country in respect and obedience but render to God your first loyalty—the things that are God's. Love your family, but put Me first in your heart. Then you can love them more fully.

MONDAY   St. John 18:33-36; Hebrews 12:2

Looking to Jesus the pioneer and perfecter of our faith, who for the joy that was set before him endured the cross, despising the shame, and is seated at the right hand of the throne of God.   Hebrews 12:2

My Kingship is not dependent on worldly power but it is the Power of God at work in this world. I could have sent legions of angels to protect Me from Pilate's verdict so that I would not have been crucified. But I freely embraced the Cross—for without the shedding of My Blood there could have been no salvation of the world. For the joy that was set before Me, I endured all the degradation and suffering that man could put upon Me—for your sake! Will you let this present dying to self make you more usable in this world to glorify the King of Kings?

TUESDAY   St. John 18:37-40; 1:1-18

But to all who received him, who believed in his name, he gave power to become children of God.   St. John 1:12

I have been in the Godhead from the foundation of the world—but I came in the lowly form of a man, born in a stable. Jealous men, with Pilate's sanction, crucified Me on a cross which bore the label, "The King of the Jews." I came into the world to bear witness to the Truth: to set men free. The world did not receive Me then, and it does not receive Me yet. But you have received Me. When you lift Me up in your lives, others will be drawn to Me. Those who are of the Truth will hear My Voice speaking through you, bearing witness in their hearts.

WEDNESDAY   Romans 14:6-9

If we live, we live to the Lord, and if we die, we die to the Lord; so then, whether we live or whether we die, we are the Lord's.   Romans 14:8

No one of you is an island unto himself: for whatever you do or think or say, you influence someone else. Therefore, if you eat, eat to the glory of God—not out of gluttony. If you abstain, do so in thankfulness to God, not out of pride in your own self-discipline. Living or dying makes no difference: if you live, let it be to the glory of God; if you die, you return to Him. In My death and resurrection, I became Lord of the dead as well as of the living. In life or in death, you belong to Me, Beloved, for you have committed yourself totally to be Mine.

THURSDAY   Galatians 2:20

I have been crucified with Christ; it is no longer I who live, but Christ who lives in me; and the life I now live in the flesh I live by faith in the Son of God, who loved me and gave himself for me.   Galatians 2:20

You have died to the legalisms and hypocrisies of the past so that you might live unto Me. You have been nailed to the Cross with Me through your confession of sin and surrender of self-will. You have identified your life with Me. It is hard for the world to comprehend this mystery: that you no longer live but that *I live in you!* The life you now live is a witness to My glory. By faith in My Love, in My Power to overcome death, you have died to self-will to be reborn into New Life. You now live in a new dimension: the Power of My Love now transforms your life.

FRIDAY Galatians 5:24-26

If we live by the Spirit, let us also walk by the Spirit.
Galatians 5:25

The fleshly passions have been crucified in those of you who truly belong to Me. Therefore walk by My Spirit, not depending on worldly crutches. You do not need other spirits to give you a lift. Live by My Spirit, not by your former standards and habit patterns. Do not covet another's gifts or possessions. Do not stir up trouble with others. And beware of pride in yourself for this is the first and last sin of the saints. Let the fruit of My Spirit grow to maturity in you.

SATURDAY Isaiah 8:19-22; Acts 16:16-24

And when they say to you, "Consult the mediums and the wizards who chirp and mutter," should not a people consult their God? Should they consult the dead on behalf of the living? Isaiah 8:19

There are many today who are disobediently seeking to know the future so that they can amass greater fortunes or manipulate people. They are listening to false spirits—divining spirits that are not divine, but Satanic. They open themselves to the occult, often in ignorance of My Word. But *ignorance is no excuse* for the Christian who is committed to walk by My Spirit! Paul cast out the deceitful spirit from a slave girl who was used by fortune-tellers as a medium. He was jailed because of false charges by her owners. I am grieved today to see My people consulting mediums and sorcerers. They contact deceiving spirits who impersonate the dead. You must warn them of this evil before it is too late.

SUNDAY   Philippians 1:19-24

My desire is to depart and be with Christ, for that is far better.   Philippians 1:23b

My servant Paul was not afraid of death because he knew that when he departed, he would be with Me. Why are you fearful for your loved one? She has lived to My glory in this life. She has labored faithfully and is ready to be called home. Until now she has been needed here for your sakes. But now she is very weary of this life. She has walked in My Spirit here. How much more will be her Joy—her gain—as she steps through the doorway of death into My nearer, continuous Presence. Release her. Rejoice that she will be with Me soon —forever!

MONDAY   James 1:9-12

Blessed is the man who endures trial, for when he has stood the test he will receive the crown of life which God has promised to those who love him.   James 1:12

My children, all of you must face the test of life. But what matters is the Spirit which leads your spirit. Rich or poor, proud or humble, you will all pass away from the trials and temptations of this life. To those of you who have stood the test and resisted the enemy, there will be the heavenly crown of eternal life. You who have risen above these trials will be blessed, for your love has been proven in the fire. The promise of the Father is to all those who love Him and keep His commandments. *Remain faithful to Me*—no matter how great the trial may be.

TUESDAY James 1:13-18

Let no one say when he is tempted, "I am tempted by God"; for God cannot be tempted with evil and he himself tempts no one. James 1:13

When you are tempted, it is the evil one who is trying to sabotage your relationship with Me and with My other children. Do not blame the Father for this temptation. It is your own desire that tempts you to disobey. The temptation must be resisted quickly lest you succumb to it. If you dally with it, your will becomes weak and you are ready to sin. Do not let the devil deceive you as he did Job at first. There is no variableness in the Father. He gives only good gifts to His children. Where He tests you, it is only to see whether you need more growth before you can be given more responsibility. You are called to be the fruit of His new covenant with mankind: to be strong in His Truth.

WEDNESDAY I John 1:8-10; Ephesians 1:7

In him we have redemption through his blood, the forgiveness of our trespasses, according to the riches of his grace. Ephesians 1:7

Do not be discouraged when at times you slip back a little. Even the growth of plants and trees is in spurts. Ask My forgiveness the moment you realize your slippage of commitment. Offer this area in repentance and ask not only for My forgiveness but also for grace to be kept from failing again. Let Me unmess the situation. *Release* it to Me to repair the damage. You will be amazed at the good I can bring forth from it. *Be forgiving of yourself now*—even as I have forgiven you.

THURSDAY   Romans 3:23-28; St. Matthew 26:41

For we hold that a man is justified by faith apart from works of law.   Romans 3:28

To be complacent about your sins is not the same as to be patient with yourself while I am bringing forth victory in this area of your life. No one should be complacent. All of you have sinned and fallen short of My glory. But, likewise, all of you can be restored by faith in My grace. Berating yourself only gives power to the enemy. Claim My Power to bring victory in this situation! Then refrain from putting yourself again in the place where you know that you will be subjected to heavy temptation. Let your will and actions be coordinated with your prayers for My help.

FRIDAY   Philippians 3:12-16

I press on toward the goal for the prize of the upward call of God in Christ Jesus.   Philippians 3:14

My child, now that you have asked and been given My forgiveness, *accept it with thanksgiving.* I have wiped the slate of life clean! The dirty chalkmarks of self-condemnation

(guilt) and condemnation by others are now no longer binding you, for I have erased them—along with Satan's accusations. Give this whole situation to Me. If you have not now
forgiven yourself, you are pretending to be God: you are setting up your own judgment as higher than Mine. Forget what
lies behind you and press on. I have much for you to do. I
can weave this into the tapestry of life. Be humble and forgiving to others who also stumble.

SATURDAY Philippians 4:19-20

*And my God will supply every need of yours according
to his riches in glory in Christ Jesus.* Philippians 4:19

Why are you anxious about this need, My child? Do you
believe that I have limitless resources? When you stop
fretting and worrying, I can supply every need according to
My riches. Praise changes things; but it changes you also. Be
willing to let Me make the changes in your life as necessary.
Pray with thanksgiving in advance about *all* your needs—
physical, spiritual, financial.

SUNDAY II Corinthians 4:7-12

*But we have this treasure in earthen vessels, to show that
the transcendent power belongs to God and not to us.*
II Corinthians 4:7

You are only the vessel in which My Power is manifested.
When My transcendent Love abides in you, nothing can crush
you nor make you despair. Afflictions and persecutions may

come your way, but they will not overcome you as long as you let My risen Life manifest itself through you. My disciples, while you are dying more and more to self, you are increasing more and more in My Resurrection Life. Do not fall a prey to discouragement, but rejoice in each trial as you lift it to Me.

MONDAY II Corinthians 4:17-5:5

Because we look not to the things that are seen but to the things that are unseen; for the things that are seen are transient, but the things that are unseen are eternal. II Corinthians 4:18

Do not fear death of the body which is only an earthly covering, for you will receive a spiritual body when this one is no longer needed. You have received the Spirit of God as a guarantee of your salvation. Have no anxiety: for death of this body will be swallowed up in an eternal life of glory which the Father has prepared for you, His beloved children. Look not to the seen things that will pass away but rather to the unseen, the eternal.

TUESDAY Isaiah 53:3-5

But he was wounded for our transgressions, he was bruised for our iniquities; upon him was the chastisement that made us whole, and with his stripes we are healed. Isaiah 53:5

In your present suffering, My child, you have not yet been bruised as I was for your sakes. I was wounded for your disobedience and took punishment so that you might not have to bear the brunt of your sins. I was despised by the authorities and forsaken even by My friends when man's jealousy condemned me to die for you and for all mankind. Will you not gladly live for Me?

WEDNESDAY St. Mark 11:25

And whenever you stand praying, forgive, if you have anything against any one; so that your Father also who is in heaven may forgive you your trespasses. St. Mark 11:25

Can you not forgive this loved one who has hurt you so deeply? I, too, suffered betrayal by one very close to Me. I had to watch Judas go out into the night, although I knew what he was about to do. I could warn him, but I could not change his heart. As I now forgive you of your sins, you must forgive her. You cannot pray effective prayers if you hold this bitterness in your heart. It will sear your soul and harden your spirit and cripple your body. Pray to be able to forgive her—even as I forgive you.

THURSDAY Psalm 107:17-20

Then they cried to the Lord in their trouble, and he delivered them from their distress. Psalm 107:19

Often illness is caused by sin which separates you from Me. Pray (when you are ill) to be shown any secret fear or resentment, any critical or self-pitying spirit, that may be a cause of your illness. Claim My Power to deliver you in your time of trouble. Do not fix this illness upon yourself as "my arthritis" but claim My healing—regardless of the stiffness or pain. Forgive those who have hurt you in the past and those of whom you have been critical. There is healing power in My Love. Let it flow through your body, mind and spirit.

FRIDAY   Romans 10:14-17

How beautiful are the feet of those who preach good news!   Romans 10:15b

You are not called to preach doom but the Good News of My saving grace, My healing and transforming Power. Faith comes through hearing the message of the Word of God. Will you be one who will take this message to those who cannot call upon Me because they have never believed in Me? How can they trust in Me if they have never really heard My Voice? Will you be the one sent? You can preach My gospel in the byways of life: you can proclaim My healing love to those in need.

SATURDAY   Hebrews 11:6

And without faith it is impossible to please him. For whoever would draw near to God must believe that he exists and that he rewards those who seek him.   Hebrews 11:6

Your witness today to one in doubt can be like a beacon in the night of despair. This person wants to believe that I am Reality, but he has been discouraged. Help him to have the faith to seek Me with earnestness. Help him to catch fire in faith. Believe for him—until he can be believed into believing in My Love and Power.

SUNDAY   Hebrews 11:1; St. Matthew 4:23-24

And he went about all Galilee, teaching in their synagogues and preaching the gospel of the kingdom and healing every disease and every infirmity among the people.   St. Matthew 4:23

In My earthly ministry, My healing Power was manifested over and over again. There were no incurables for Me. My Touch has still its ancient Power. Will you bring this one in faith that he will be healed? Will you continue to hold him up to Me in prayers of thanksgiving? Will you let Me consecrate your imagination so that you can see in your mind's eye a picture of him whole? I need your faith as the substance, the conviction, of a reality that is to come.

MONDAY   St. John 20:26-29

Have you believed because you have seen me? Blessed are those who have not seen and yet believe.   St. John 20:29b

When you believe expectantly (without seeing Me at work in the situation), you are passing a test that even My disciple Thomas once failed. Sometimes I test your faith to see the depth of your commitment. Those who are easily discouraged will not make good "prayer warriors" in today's world. *Regardless of circumstances*, claim Me as your *Lord over all!* Today I opened for you a way where there was no way through those clouds and your plane landed safely. *Rejoice* in My Power!

TUESDAY   Hebrews 13:8

Jesus Christ is the same yesterday and today and for ever. Hebrews 13:8

Do you believe that I am the same—in all your yesterdays? I have loved you when you were rejected by others, protected you when you were endangered by others, guided you when you were confused by others. My Love for you is constant, unchanging, unconditional. I am with you *now* in this disheartening situation. Claim My Power to rule in it—to overrule the enemy who is trying to distract your gaze from Me. I shall be with you in all your tomorrows. *Trust* in Me *NOW*.

WEDNESDAY   Psalm 94:16-19

When the cares of my heart are many, thy consolations cheer my soul.   Psalm 94:19

My protection has kept your foot from slipping in this difficult walk when Satan was trying to block your passage. You have been faithful to My guidance and My Love has supported you in these two days of testing. The burdens have been heavy upon you, but My strength has enabled you to carry out this mission. My Love enfolds you now. Let Me console you when those who are jealous rise up against you. Let My Joy be your strength.

THURSDAY   Jeremiah 32:27, 37-41

Behold, I am the Lord, the God of all flesh; is anything too hard for me?   Jeremiah 32:27

When your people are being scattered by the enemy's attacks, remember that I am still God of all flesh. What can be too difficult for the Lord? I will bring them back to this place of safety. I will unite them with one heart and one purpose. Out of their brokenness over this hurt to their pride will come a new strength.

FRIDAY   Numbers 11:23

And the Lord said to Moses, "Is the Lord's hand shortened? Now you shall see whether my word will come true for you or not."   Numbers 11:23

When I proved Myself to My servant Moses, My arm was not shortened. Can you not trust Me to bring My Word to pass? I have given you My prophecy concerning this situation where the wolves—the ravening wolves—have been attacking the lambs. My words shall be fulfilled. *Hold fast to My promises.* What I have done this day will be continued in the days to come and My Church shall be healed. Rejoice in the fullness of My Power at work among My people.

SATURDAY   St. Matthew 13:3-9

He who has ears, let him hear.   St. Matthew 13:9

The poor soil, My children, refers to many people all about you in today's world. They are those impoverished souls who starve spiritually while trying to live a high standard materially or intellectually. They follow Me as a new diversion. But when the testings come into their lives, they quickly fall away: there is no root of faith. Do not be discouraged in your prayer ministry. Your prayer group is like the field. Some of the seeds you sow will be devoured by the enemy: for the ground of their hearts will be like a path—too hardened to hear. Some will be too choked with busy-ness. But the good soil will bring forth fruit. Be patient, be persevering in sowing.

SUNDAY   St. Matthew 23:10-12

He who is greatest among you shall be your servant.   St. Matthew 23:11

My child, you have been set on a pedestal at times by members of your family or prayer group or Church. Do not let people put their God-images on you. Your calling is to help them find a vision of Me—to *exalt Me as Master,* so that I can truly bless them and guide their lives. You cannot "play God," for your own feet are of clay. When they try to exalt you, turn them to Me as the Source. As you humble yourself, I will be exalted in you. The greatest shall become the least. The humble shall be used mightily in My Kingdom.

MONDAY   St. Luke 14:7-11

For every one who exalts himself will be humbled, and he who humbles himself will be exalted.   St. Luke 14:11

Do not choose the work in your Church that brings human glory. Choose the lower seats. Let *Me* call you to come up higher as I see that you are ready. Do not choose the most advanced ministry out of pride or impatience. Be willing to be faithful in service: visit the sick even when you do not want to go; be a faithful member of the small prayer group, even when it is dwindling and you want to go to a more "successful" one. That is your "battle station." I count on *you* to be there to resist the enemy—to help the weak to resist him. I need to be able to *depend on your faithfulness* before I can open doors of higher ministry to you!

TUESDAY   St. Luke 18:9-14

For every one who exalts himself will be humbled, but he who humbles himself will be exalted.   St. Luke 18:14b

When you pray, Beloved, do not pray like the publican: do not count your virtues or gifts in self-righteousness. Do not scorn someone with lesser talents. Do not justify yourself. You cannot earn your salvation by good works. Come to Me in true humility—knowing that you yourself are not worthy but that *I* am worthy and merciful to forgive. If you exalt yourself, you will be humbled: the repentant sinner will enter My Kingdom before the self-righteous.

WEDNESDAY   St. Matthew 5:6; St. John 21:15-17

He said to him the third time, "Simon, son of John, do you love me?" Peter was grieved because he said to him the third time, "Do you love me?" And he said to him, "Lord, you know everything; you know that I love you." Jesus said to him, "Feed my sheep."   St. John 21:17

Many of My children are hungering and thirsting for more of My Righteousness. They need to be fed by My Love. When

I called Peter to feed My sheep and My lambs, it was a sign
that he had been forgiven. When I asked Peter if he loved Me,
I gave him that commission. I give it to you now—today.

THURSDAY   St. Matthew 5:3,5

*Blessed are the poor in spirit, for theirs is the kingdom of
heaven.*   St. Matthew 5:3

Those who are poor in spirit are humble enough to enter
into My Kingdom through the low door. Those who are not
proud but meek in heart will be My children and will inherit
as sons and daughters of the King. Do not strive amongst yourselves for worldly positions of honor. My Kingdom is not of
this world, but can be *in this world*—as you build on the foundation of My Love.

FRIDAY   St. Luke 14:12-15

*But when you give a feast, invite the poor, the maimed, the
lame, the blind, and you will be blessed, because they cannot repay you. You will be repaid at the resurrection of the
just.*   St. Luke 14:13-14

Do not try to seek out the great, but rather the poor and
lowly in heart. If you do good to those who will repay you,
there is no virtue in your giving. Give because you have received from Me. Give to the weak, the sick, the broken. Give
to them out of the abundance of My Love and you shall be
blessed—for you shall share in the Kingdom of God. Give the

broken bread and the pressed wine as My Spirit is poured out through you: a living sacrifice, to My glory.

SATURDAY   St. Matthew 18:1-6

Truly, I say to you, unless you turn and become like children, you will never enter the kingdom of heaven. St. Matthew 18:3 (in part)

Many of you are afraid to be *childlike* and yet I have told you that you could not enter into My Kingdom unless you became as trusting, guileless and expectant as a little child. The proud will be left outside while the humble shall be admitted. Beware that you do not cause a child of Mine to stumble, for your punishment will be terrible. To discipline a child *in love* is wise and loving. But to be vindictive or sadistic, to be cruel or deceptive, to lead a child into sin or evil, is to deny Me.

SUNDAY   St. Matthew 18:7-10a

Woe to the world for temptations to sin! For it is necessary that temptations come, but woe to the man by whom the temptation comes! St. Matthew 18:7

Temptations come to all, for the devil is at work in the world causing men and women to sin. If you sin, you have need to be forgiven. But when you cause another to sin, you are in double peril. Cut out of your life anything that keeps you in bondage to sin. Do not cause a child to feel despised, lest you destroy the man within him. Do not bind a child in criticism lest he become the very person you do not want him to be.

MONDAY St. Matthew 18:10-14

So it is not the will of my Father who is in heaven that one of these little ones should perish. St. Matthew 18:14

Many of you have forgotten that the angels of heaven do the Father's bidding. They have brought good news to some and protection to others of My children. Do not think that your actions will go unnoticed when you despise the little ones who are too helpless to defend themselves. Their angels are watching over them. The Father knows and repays injustice in His timing. He seeks the sheep that is lost. It is not His will for the innocent and weak to suffer injustice. It is man's mis-use of his God-given freedom of will.

TUESDAY Psalm 91:7-13

For he will give his angels charge of you to guard you in all your ways. Psalm 91:11

Can you not believe the Scriptures that promise help from My angels in time of need? Angels foretold My birth, and they ministered to Me after the devil tempted Me in the wilderness. If you believe, My angels can help to guard you in all your ways. If you make your secret place of refuge in the shadow of the Almighty, you will be kept safely in time of danger. Many of My servants have experienced this; their sole trust is in Me.

WEDNESDAY Psalm 91:14-15

When he calls to me, I will answer him; I will be with him in trouble, I will rescue him and honor him. Psalm 91:15

This protection is not a result of mere good works. It is not because of lip-service to Me. When you truly cleave to Me in love, I can hedge you about with My protective armor. When you call to Me in expectant faith, I can direct your paths to safety. The quality of your faith and love create a state of receptivity that enables Me to work more victoriously in the circumstances of your life.

THURSDAY St. Matthew 5:22; 7:1-3

Judge not, that you be not judged. St. Matthew 7:1

Some of you have taken too lightly My commands about loving your brother. My judgment will be upon those who are angry with a person and those who call another person a fool. You may be angry at the *sin*. You may condemn the sin, the danger, the foolishness, the waste, or the cruelty, but only the Father can be the Judge of men! *Only the Father can condemn the sinner.* Beware lest you sin by condemnation—as greatly as the person you have condemned.

FRIDAY Isaiah 30:1-2

"Woe to the rebellious children," says the Lord, "who carry out a plan, but not mine." Isaiah 30:1a

Many of you today are like the rebellious children of Israel who made their own plans and then expected Me to bless and fulfill them. You must pray earnestly to *know My Will*. Before you begin this undertaking, pray to know *if* it is My Will, My highest Will. Pray to know when and how and by whom My Will shall be accomplished. Cover each detail by faith with My Blood. Ask for explicit guidance and for protection from the deceits of the Satanic forces that try to block My Plans. *Claim* My protection.

SATURDAY   Isaiah 30:15

For thus said the Lord God, the Holy One of Israel, "In returning and rest you shall be saved; in quietness and in trust shall be your strength." And you would not.   Isaiah 30:15

You say that you are too busy to take time to pray in such detail—but it will save you time and grief and failure if you see to it that *My* Plans are in the making and not just your own! Put your daily calendar under the protection of My Blood. *Rest* in the new liberty of My Spirit. You shall be saved by turning back from your own motivations and schemings. *Trusting in Me* will be the source of your strength. You shall then be quiet in your inner being—no matter how great the outer turmoil.

SUNDAY   Isaiah 30:18

Therefore the Lord waits to be gracious to you; therefore he exalts himself to show mercy to you. For the Lord is a God of justice; blessed are all those who wait for him. Isaiah 30:18

Can you not believe that the Father will exalt Himself and show you His mercy in this situation? You feel utterly incompetent—but it is *not you* who must change defeat into victory! My people in this Church have been humbled by the failure of one whom I had called to be a leader of the sheep. They are hungry to be fed by the Truth, the living reality of My Scriptures claimed expectantly today in their great needs. Go to them as to My lambs. Feed them with My Word. Touch them for Me. My justice shall rest upon all of those who wait upon Me. My Power shall flow through you to meet their needs.

MONDAY   Isaiah 33:2

> *O Lord, be gracious to us; we wait for thee. Be our arm every morning, our salvation in the time of trouble.*   Isaiah 33:2

You have waited upon Me each morning and I have given you My grace for the day. Come to Me daily in the early morning hours. Let Me be your arm extended to help others today. Let Me be your salvation in times of difficulty. Let Me be your wholeness in times of need.

TUESDAY   Isaiah 58:7-9

> *Then you shall call, and the Lord will answer; you shall cry, and he will say, Here I am.*   Isaiah 58:9a

Because you have shared your bread (spiritual and physical) with the hungry, I am answering your call. You have brought home to My Love the poor, the wandering, the wounded and the naked in spirit. My healing has sprung forth quickly in you. My glory shall follow you, even as your right use of My gift of life has gone before you. When you call upon Me, Beloved, I shall answer.

WEDNESDAY II Corinthians 4:3-5

For what we preach is not ourselves, but Jesus Christ as Lord, with ourselves as your servants for Jesus' sake. II Corinthians 4:5

There are far too many unbelievers who have been blinded by the prince of this world. They cannot see the light of My Truth. The Good News is veiled to them for they cannot see My glory. You are to preach and teach My Gospel. For My sake, you will be a servant to many.

THURSDAY Isaiah 58:9b-11

If you take away from the midst of you the yoke, the pointing of the finger, and speaking wickedness, if you pour yourself out for the hungry and satisfy the desire of the afflicted, then shall your light rise in the darkness and your gloom be as the noonday. Isaiah 58:9b-10

You are to pour yourself out for the weak and hungry, the sick and distressed. You are to stop those who would speak evil or critical or slandering words. In obedience, follow My commissioning. Then I shall guide you continuously and give you health and light even in the dark moments of your life. You shall be unfailing like a spring and peaceful like a watered garden.

FRIDAY   Romans 7:14-25a

Thanks be to God through Jesus Christ our Lord!   Romans 7:25a

Some of you have been puzzled because the carnal man has been warring against the spiritual man. You do not understand your own actions in this instance. You find yourselves in conflict—doing the things that you don't want to do and failing to do the things that you want. You know what is right but you cannot do it—for the carnal man still has dominion in your life. Let Me take dominion *now*. Your dying unto self-will opens the door to My Victory in your life.

SATURDAY   Romans 8:1-6

There is therefore now no condemnation for those who are in Christ Jesus.   Romans 8:1

My Spirit has power to set you free from the carnal man so that you are no longer bound by the old law of sin and death. For you who walk according to the Spirit (instead of being under the old dominion of your fleshly desires, habits and reactions), there is a new liberty and joy! This liberty is not license—it is the discipline of the Spirit who enables you to set your minds, to center your lives, on God's higher things. It is Life and Peace, My children.

SUNDAY   Romans 8:7-9

But you are not in the flesh, you are in the Spirit, if the Spirit of God really dwells in you.   Romans 8:9a

Some of you are claiming the indwelling Spirit, but your walk is obviously not free of the fleshly defeats. You are still leaning on your old crutches instead of submitting these desires to God so that you can be set free. If My Spirit truly dwells in you, there will be freedom from old bondages—mental, emotional and physical. Your relationships will be changed as My Spirit abides in you. If you are still clinging to the carnal man, let go—for no amount of good works will take the place of real surrender. *Unless My Spirit abides in you,* you are no Christian.

MONDAY   James 2:17-26

For as the body apart from the spirit is dead, so faith apart from works is dead.   James 2:26

When you are truly surrendered to Me in spirit, your faith will be used to help bring forth greater works. Good works alone are not sufficient, but faith is reinforced by works. Abraham offered his son Isaac: because his faith was so strong, his works acted it out. Abraham's faith in God was completed by his acts. Will you let your good works be the acting out of your faith today? Will you put shoes of action on your prayers for others? Let your faith proceed into works.

TUESDAY   James 4:1-2

You do not have, because you do not ask.   James 4:2c

Covetousness has slipped into your group. This bickering is the deceit of the enemy trying to stir up trouble amongst you. Wars and quarrelings are caused by jealousy and greed. You need to *ask* for My Power in order to have it. You need to *claim* My victory rather than to quarrel over whose ministry is more important. Be not envious of one another but *complete* each other's ministry in My Love.

WEDNESDAY   James 4:3-6

God opposes the proud, but gives grace to the humble. James 4:6b

Your petitions have been prayed in the wrong spirit at times. You do not have to justify yourself to anyone else. You do not have to justify or defend Me. My choices are not the world's choices. The Father yearns over His children and He gives grace to the humble—those who are open and willing to be led by Him! He holds back the proud who try to achieve good works without the indwelling of My Spirit. Be faithful to Me. Let your prayers be prayed *in My Spirit*, not just My Name.

THURSDAY   Hebrews 12:1-2

Therefore, since we are surrounded by so great a cloud of witnesses, let us also lay aside every weight, and sin which clings so closely, and let us run with perseverance the race that is set before us.   Hebrews 12:1

My saints are to lay aside the weights and sins that have been woven so deeply into the past, especially those sins that cling so closely. I have called you to a race—not a tea party. You are to *bask in My Love*, but only so that you can run the race—*with perseverance!* When the enemy strikes, you are not to give up so easily. I despised shame and bore the agony of the Cross—for the joy of the future with My Father. Can you not bear with Me a little while?

FRIDAY   Hebrews 12:3-4

Consider him who endured from sinners such hostility against himself, so that you may not grow weary or faint-hearted.   Hebrews 12:3

When you feel sorry for yourself because the devil is attacking this particular work you are doing, look to Me. I am the author of your faith and I will bring it into greater fruitfulness as you *gaze on Me*—so that you will not grow weary or discouraged. I will perfect your spirit to enable you to resist sin and the devil. You have been assaulted, but *you* have not yet shed your blood!

SATURDAY   Hebrews 12:11-12

For the moment all discipline seems painful rather than pleasant; later it yields the peaceful fruit of righteousness to those who have been trained by it.   Hebrews 12:11

During this pressure of important work My discipline seems painful, but it will not always be so. Accept the testings of life. Accept them *patiently* and *cheerfully* in the awareness of My Love. The fruit shall be borne from lives of righteousness to those who have been trained by discipline to *trust in Me.*

SUNDAY   Hebrews 12:7-13

It is for discipline that you have to endure. God is treating you as sons; for what son is there whom his father does not discipline?   Hebrews 12:7

Too many of My children hate discipline. They want the fruit of the Spirit—Love, Joy and Peace—but *without* the discipline! Only those who have truly come the way of the Cross will be usable in My higher service. The others will drop out too quickly. Lift your hands and voices to Me in prayer. Strengthen your commitment so that whatever is weak in you may be healed through this testing. Rejoice in this discipline of your spirit.

MONDAY   St. Matthew 8:1-4

Lord, if you will, you can make me clean.   St. Matthew 8:2b

When you pray for yourself or for others, pray for *wholeness.* I am concerned about your whole personality. My healing is much more than getting well physically. My healing touch is upon all your relationships as well as your mind and spirit. When they are in harmony with My Will for you for wholeness, miracles will happen. I say to you as to the leper of old, "Be thou made whole." *Act* upon your faith—now!

TUESDAY   St. Matthew 8:5-13

Go; be it done for you as you have believed.   St. Matthew 8:13 (in part)

You have come to Me now as the centurion came on behalf of his servant. I now speak the word of authority for your loved one. Do you have the faith to claim this healing as the Roman soldier did? Do you have his humility in your heart? *Believe* that this healing is taking place. It shall be done according to your faith.

WEDNESDAY St. Matthew 8:16-17

He took our infirmities and bore our diseases. St. Matthew 8:17b

My servant Isaiah spoke a prophecy that I would bear your diseases and heal your infirmities. Do you believe it? Will you claim this reality in your own illness? Let Me cast out this spirit of fear that is possessing you. Let Me banish this anxiety over your loved one. You cannot intercede with faith when you are consumed with fear.

THURSDAY St. Matthew 8:14-15

He touched her hand, and the fever left her, and she rose and served him. St. Matthew 8:15

When I touched the hand of Peter's mother-in-law, she was instantly healed of a fever. Her response was to rise up and serve Me. Do you want to turn back to the old self-centered, carnal way of living? Or do you want to be made whole to be capable of serving Me?

FRIDAY St. Matthew 9:1-8

"But that you may know that the Son of man has authority on earth to forgive sins"—he then said to the paralytic—"Rise, take up your bed and go home." St. Matthew 9:6

Like the paralytic, your sins are causing this distress—sins of resentment, fear and self-pity. They will hurt *you* more than the person you resent. Your fears paralyze you so that you are not able to see clearly My solution to your problems. You have slipped back into the old way, but My grace is available to you now. Praise Me with all your heart. Your sins are forgiven: accept My mercy, My forgiveness now for all that you have confessed. Rise up now and *walk in My Peace.*

SATURDAY Acts 20:35

In all things I have shown you that by so toiling one must help the weak, remembering the words of the Lord Jesus, how he said, "It is more blessed to give than to receive." Acts 20:35

Now that you have experienced My Will for wholeness, you can share this precious gift of Faith and Love with others in need of My healing touch today. You have received from Me with Joy, but it is even more blessed to give forth My Love to others. Let Me touch this one in need *through you* today.

SUNDAY St. John 3:16

For God so loved the world that he gave his only Son, that whoever believes in him should not perish but have eternal life. St. John 3:16

Out of My Father's Love for the world, I came into being in the Person of Jesus of Nazareth. I was born into this world to take upon Myself the sins of mankind. For those who believe in Me, there is now opened the door of eternal Life. Help the wandering, the blind, the lost to find Me.

MONDAY St. Matthew 5:13

You are the salt of the earth; but if salt has lost its taste, how shall its saltness be restored? It is no longer good for anything except to be thrown out and trodden under foot by men. St. Matthew 5:13

You are called to be the salt of the earth. Beware lest you lose your savor and become no different from those who have not seen the Light of My Presence. Salt is a precious substance, for it brings out the flavor of other foods. When you are with others, does your presence bring out goodness and holiness in them? *Be* the salt of the earth.

TUESDAY St. Matthew 5:9

Blessed are the peacemakers, for they shall be called sons of God. St. Matthew 5:9

Pray for this whole group to be lifted into Me. Pray for My Love to iron out all the differences amongst My children. *Be* the peacemaker I can use to anoint their spirits with My Love. Send a flood tide of My Love upon them—one by one—until you see their faces relaxing and their attitudes changing. You are called to be a son of God—now.

WEDNESDAY   St. Matthew 4:3-4

Man shall not live by bread alone, but by every word that proceeds from the mouth of God. St. Matthew 4:4b

You need to be fed as a group more by My Word—My living Bread. These dissensions are of Satan. They are fed by too much discussion in your prayer group. *Stop* and *pray*— whenever humans are tempted to work out their own carnal solutions to problems. Let the group be silent to meditate on My Word, to be fed spiritually. You shall not live by physical bread or by intellect alone, My children.

THURSDAY   St. Matthew 3:1-3,11-12

I baptize you with water for repentance, but he who is coming after me is mightier than I, whose sandals I am not worthy to carry; he will baptize you with the Holy Spirit and with fire. St. Matthew 3:11

John came before Me to prepare the way through the preaching of repentance. John's baptism was one of repentance, for he proclaimed My Kingdom as nigh. But on the day of Pentecost, I baptized you with My Holy Spirit and with fire— power for ministry that My Name might be glorified in the world.

FRIDAY   Acts 1:7-8; 2:1-4

But you shall receive power when the Holy Spirit has come upon you; and you shall be my witnesses in Jerusalem and in all Judea and Samaria and to the end of the earth. Acts 1:8

When My fire fell upon My disciples at Pentecost, it was a fulfillment of the prophecy I gave them before My ascension.

The Spirit could not be given until I was ascended and glorified. But now *you* have received this most precious Gift of My Holy Spirit. Do not belittle any of My gifts. Accept *all* that I give you in praise, in humility, in wonder at the depths of My Love for you.

SATURDAY Acts 1:8; St. Matthew 23:37-39; Psalm 122:6

Blessed is he who comes in the name of the Lord. St. Matthew 23:39b

Some of you have been My witnesses in Jerusalem. Some of you know My heartache—how I wept for the city and would have gathered her into My arms. Today she is in travail and no man knows the outcome. Pray for the Peace of Jerusalem. Pray for the conversion of the Jewish people. Pray for *all* the nations of the world that My Peace may rest upon them. *Be My channel* of intercession today.

SUNDAY Philippians 4:11-13

I can do all things in him who strengthens me. Philippians 4:13

As you grow more totally committed, My children, you will find that circumstances have less power over you. As My Love increases, you will be less affected by material needs or even the opinions of others. You will be content—in plenty or in poverty, while you are being used mightily or in times of waiting on Me in secret. My abiding Presence is the secret of Life.

MONDAY   Romans 16:25-27

To the only wise God be glory for evermore through Jesus Christ! Amen.   Romans 16:27

Through the prophetic writings there was foretold My coming into life as God made man. This mystery (which was so long a secret) has been manifested to bring about obedience to the Father. What the Law could not do, My death and resurrection have accomplished: so that by faith in Me, men could become obedient to their Creator. Proclaim this Good News in your lives. Share it with those who lack faith.

TUESDAY   Romans 8:14-17

For all who are led by the Spirit of God are sons of God. Romans 8:14

Proclaim the spirit of sonship to those who have been in slavery to a spirit of fear! Tell them the *Good News* that no matter how great the problem, they can cry "Abba" to the Eternal Father who has called them to be His children, heirs of the King of Creation! Comfort them in those times of suffering and rejection that the world metes out to them: for if you suffer with and for Me, you will also be glorified with Me.

WEDNESDAY   Ephesians 3:20-21

Now to him who by the power at work within us is able to do far more abundantly than all that we ask or think, to him be glory in the church and in Christ Jesus to all generations, for ever and ever. Amen.   Ephesians 3:20-21

My children, when you pray, remember that the Father is able to do abundantly *more* than you can even ask for since He created those whom you love. He loves them far *more* than you can ever love in your finite beings. Pray that His Power will be at work in the Church. Pray in My Name and to the glory of God. Pray in awareness of His Almighty, Eternal Love. Pray in joyous thanksgiving—not in fear!

THURSDAY   St. John 8:14-16

Yet even if I do judge, my judgment is true, for it is not I alone that judge, but I and he who sent me.   St. John 8:16

My Father and I are one and our judgment is not man's judgment of situations. I came not to judge but to save mankind. I came from the Godhead and I returned to sit at the right hand of the Father—to intercede for sinners who in this life are making false choices. When you judge, your judgment is of the flesh: you lack divine wisdom and knowledge and mercy. Can you not *trust Us* to save all that *want* to be saved? Those who do not want to be saved would be miserable in Heaven in God's Presence where the whole company is praising Him day and night.

FRIDAY Proverbs 3:1-8; St. Matthew 25:41-46

Be not wise in your own eyes; fear the Lord, and turn away from evil. Proverbs 3:7

Those who hate God are disobedient to His commandments. My son, write His commandments on the slate of your heart so that you will keep them in love, not out of duty. Be loyal to Him who gives you the precious gift of Life—in the present and for eternity. Your human wisdom and understanding are lacking: trust in Me to make your paths straight. Turn your back on the paths of evil as you commit your life to Me. I will bring healing and wholeness to your body and spirit. Those who in this life have not obediently followed Me will not want to be with Me for eternity. The choice is theirs: *you cannot force them to be saved.* Pray for them.

SATURDAY Galatians 5:1

For freedom Christ has set us free; stand fast therefore, and do not submit again to a yoke of slavery. Galatians 5:1

You have been set free from this sin by My Grace, but the temptation still remains as long as you consider it thus. The power of sin has been broken in you but you still have freedom of choice. Wherever possible, remove from your life these circumstances that tempt you. *Stand fast in your resolve:* do not even consider yielding! The yoke has been removed: do not put yourself back under it. *Hold fast in victory* as your desires are being changed.

SUNDAY Colossians 1:24-29

> *Him we proclaim, warning every man and teaching every man in all wisdom, that we may present every man mature in Christ.* Colossians 1:28

Some have twisted My words to satisfy their own concepts of justice. It is not true that all will be saved although I died to save all: they can choose to hear the proclamation of My saving grace or they can deny what I have made available to them—salvation, wholeness. *You* cannot decide who will be saved. No human being ever knows the last thoughts of another person. But you can proclaim the Good News. You can warn, you can teach, you can pray for them to know that their hope of glory is in Me.

MONDAY Hebrews 13:4-12

> *So Jesus also suffered outside the gate in order to sanctify the people through his own blood.* Hebrews 13:12

Today there are many false teachings concerning marriage. There are many who lust after sex, money, food, pleasure. The Father alone will judge, but He will not forsake those who trust in Him. Look to the Word of God; listen only to those who live by grace—those who accept My sacrifice as their enabling Power released through the shedding of My Blood.

TUESDAY Galatians 1:3-4; Titus 3:1-7

> *But when the goodness and loving kindness of God our Savior appeared, he saved us, not because of deeds done by*

us in righteousness, but in virtue of his own mercy, by the washing of regeneration and renewal in the Holy Spirit. Titus 3:4-5

When you see others going astray, do not become self-righteous! You yourselves were once foolishly disobedient in one way or another and I have been patient with you! Be prayerfully led to witness to those who are slaves to their destructive passions. Speak the Truth to them as I open the way. Be patiently persistent but *only in My Love*, not in judgment. You were saved not by your own good works but by the washing and renewing of My Holy Spirit—by amazing grace.

WEDNESDAY   I Timothy 6:10-16

For the love of money is the root of all evils; it is through this craving that some have wandered away from the faith and pierced their hearts with many pangs. I Timothy 6:10

My children, beware of the love of money lest it lead you away from Me. Be steadfast, gentle, loving. Life is a battle-ground and faith must be *used* if it is to increase. You have confessed your faith in Me: hold fast in right use of your God-given gifts. Shun the things that might weaken your commitment. Give honor and glory to the Father whom no man has seen. Pray for My early return.

THURSDAY   St. Mark 13:3-8

For nation will rise against nation, and kingdom against kingdom; there will be earthquakes in various places, there

will be famines; this is but the beginning of the sufferings.
St. Mark 13:8

"When will it be?" you ask. But I cannot tell you the time
—only that nation will rise up against nation, child against
parent. And the anti-Christ has already come. There will be
famines and earthquakes and many false prophets to lead you
astray. Some of you will be hated and persecuted for My sake,
but fear not. Those who persist in faith will be saved.

FRIDAY   St. Luke 18:1-8

*And will not God vindicate his elect, who cry to him day
and night? Will he delay long over them?*   St. Luke 18:7

When I come again, will I find faith? Will you be persevering, My child, no matter what the cost or the outcome
may be? Will you *pray with perseverance* like the widow before the judge? The Father will vindicate His chosen ones—
those who choose to be chosen, those who pray to Him night
and day without losing heart.

SATURDAY   St. John 17:20-26

*The glory which thou hast given me I have given to them,
that they may be one even as we are one.*   St. John 17:22

My children, when I finished the work that the Father
had given Me, I prayed not only for those early disciples but
also for all those in the future who would believe because of
their testimony. I prayed that *you* and I might be *one:* that you

might know the Love of the Father, that you might glorify His Name. I prayed that you might be kept from the evil one: that you might be with Me eternally in glory.

SUNDAY II Corinthians 11:14-15; Acts 16:16-18

For even Satan disguises himself as an angel of light. II Corinthians 11:14b

In these later days beware of those who claim to be angels of light for many have been deceived by their false teachings. Satan has his minions, his servants, who disguise themselves as they claim to be apostles of righteousness. They claim to heal, to bring good to men's minds—but in fact they condemn their souls for eternity. Those who traffic in drugs and in occult, magical experiences bring only disaster to mankind.

MONDAY Acts 10:38; Isaiah 8:19-22

How God anointed Jesus of Nazareth with the Holy Spirit and with power; how he went about doing good and healing all that were oppressed by the devil, for God was with him. Acts 10:38

In My earthly ministry, the Father anointed Me with Power to bring healing to those who were oppressed by Satan. The Oneness with the Father enabled Me to do His mighty works of healing, of Mercy, of Love. Often My Church has failed to accept this same anointing, and My people have been led to seek Satan's healers through false cults and mediums and seances. Proclaim My healing Power today.

TUESDAY St. Luke 7:11-17

God has visited his people! St. Luke 7:16c

Too many of My people do not really believe in My Power to heal the sick today. Too many do not claim My Power. They claim a "wrong diagnosis" instead of rejoicing when one of My children is healed. They fail to expect the Father to show His care for His people. They fear defeat and so fail to claim My promise in Scripture.

WEDNESDAY St. Luke 7:18-23

Go and tell John what you have seen and heard: the blind receive their sight, the lame walk, lepers are cleansed, and the deaf hear, the dead are raised up, the poor have good news preached to them. St. Luke 7:22 (in part)

When John the Baptist (in prison) sent his messengers to ask if I were the Messiah, My works of healing proved to them the answer. Deeds of mercy, acts of healing power proclaimed the Will of My Father who sent Me to be the Messiah. Those of you who have not found My healings a stumbling block, have been blessed. Those who have taken offense have denied yourselves the blessings to be received by faith. Will you *believe My promises today?*

THURSDAY St. Luke 4:18-21

The Spirit of the Lord is upon me, because he has anointed me to preach good news to the poor. He has sent me to proclaim release to the captives and recovering of sight to the blind, to set at liberty those who are oppressed, to proclaim the acceptable year of the Lord.   St. Luke 4: 18–19

When I preached in the synagogue, men marveled at My authority, for that very day the text had come true before their eyes. Will you, too, believe that I came to set captives free— those who were captive to their own sins or to the sins of others? Will you claim release for prisoners and recovery of sight for the blind when you pray for those about you in need of My healing touch today? Will you proclaim this in your daily living?

FRIDAY   St. Mark 5:35-42

Do not fear, only believe.   St. Mark 5:36b

When faith must be acted upon, it becomes real. My little prayer group—Peter, James and John—believed with Me for the healing of Jairus's daughter. My actions were of faith— claiming the Will of My Father to raise up that little girl. My words were of faith—"Fear not, only believe." My motives were of Love and Mercy. When you pray for healing, do likewise. *Be My disciples today.*

SATURDAY   St. Luke 9:1-6

And he sent them out to preach the kingdom of God and to heal.   St. Luke 9:2

My disciples went out with a twin commission—to preach the Kingdom of God and to heal the sick. They obeyed and rejoiced at My Power that was with them. When you go forth and accept hospitality in My Name, rejoice with those who believe. Where there is rejection, depart and shake the dust off your feet—but *not in resentment!* Go on to another town. Glorify only Me.

SUNDAY   Romans 13:9-14

But put on the Lord Jesus Christ, and make no provision for the flesh, to gratify its desires.   Romans 13:14

In Love, fulfill My purposes for your lives, My children. Do not sleepwalk through these eventful days! Be alert. Be clothed in My armor of Light so that you will be able to resist the subtle attacks of the enemy. Be clothed in My Love. Do not give way to immoral conduct or jealousy or bickering with one another. *Be stable in Me.*

MONDAY   Romans 2:19-25

You then who teach others, will you not teach yourself? Romans 2:21a

Some of you, who have claimed to be teachers of the uninstructed, have failed the test. You have broken the very laws you claimed to uphold. The Name of Christ has often been condemned because of the deceitful and idolatrous witness of Christians in today's world—even as My servant Paul wrote to the Jews. History repeats. Will you who use My Name today take seriously your vow to lift Me up in your daily living? Pray to see your own failures—not those of others.

TUESDAY St. Luke 9:62

Jesus said to him, "No one who puts his hand to the plow and looks back is fit for the kingdom of God." St. Luke 9:62

Many of you have eagerly taken up this new walk because you have felt the contagion of My Joy and Love in others whom I have touched as My disciples. You have gladly put your hand to the plow and with enthusiasm you have attempted to take many new steps. Will you turn back now because the going is getting rougher? Will you look back—or will you move forward? You cannot stand still!

WEDNESDAY St. Matthew 20:1-16

So the last will be first, and the first last. St. Matthew 20:16

My child, you are begrudging the recompense that one of My laborers has received. You are complaining in your heart because this one has not toiled the long hours or paid the costly price required of you. Can I not give to My children as I see their need? If you begrudge My gift to them, you may become last in My Kingdom.

THURSDAY St. Matthew 19:5-6

What therefore God has joined together, let no man put asunder. St. Matthew 19:6b

In these times, many are giving themselves lightly in marriage only to find that this is a more binding contract than they had realized. Take seriously My words. Pray for those couples who find this a hard saying. Pray for My Love to fill their hearts and join them together in holy Love. Pray for all homes to become truly centered in My Love.

FRIDAY St. Matthew 28:18-20

And Jesus came and said to them, "All authority in heaven and on earth has been given to me." St. Matthew 28:18

Do you still not believe that all authority has been given to Me? That I can take dominion over evil and bring good out of it? As these storm clouds gather, claim My authority over them. As this nation groans, claim My authority over these problems. Pray for your leaders and all those in authority. Pray for those you disapprove of—as well as those you admire.

SATURDAY Colossians 1:11-12; Galatians 3:27

May you be strengthened with all power, according to his glorious might, for all endurance and patience with joy. Colossians 1:11

My child, pray to be strengthened today with My Patience and Joy so that you may endure whatever hardships come your way. When disappointments arise, pray to be strengthened with My Power to overcome them. Like the saints who have gone on to their reward, you have been baptized into Me, putting on My Nature. Claim My Victory—not your own frustrations —as each situation arises. In time, your feelings will conform to these words.

SUNDAY Colossians 2:12-15

And you were buried with him in baptism, in which you were also raised with him through faith in the working of God, who raised him from the dead. Colossians 2:12

When you were baptized for repentance, you were buried for your sins with Me in death and raised to new life—through faith. In forgiving your sins, the Father canceled the bond for they were nailed to My Cross. No longer do Satan's principalities have power over you to defeat you. They have been disarmed. You can choose to walk in My Power triumphantly.

MONDAY St. John 1:29-34

He on whom you see the Spirit descend and remain, this is he who baptizes with the Holy Spirit. St. John 1:33b

When John baptized Me, the Spirit descended as a dove from heaven and rested on Me to fulfill the promises that I would baptize men with the Holy Spirit and with fire. Are you ready to receive this baptism for power for ministry? The Holy Spirit will lead you into all Truth. You will receive power to witness, to glorify Me. Are you ready to make this total commitment of your life?

TUESDAY St. John 4:21-30

God is spirit, and those who worship him must worship in spirit and truth. St. John 4:24

You will worship the Father in Spirit and in Truth—not in any one sanctuary but wherever you are. My Spirit will con-

vict you of many things in the past—to set you free from bondages. Like the woman by the well in Samaria, you will bear
witness to others. For My Light, shining in the darkness of
the past, will bring new cleansing in your life. There will be
a new washing and a new filling in your spirit for some of
you who are willing.

WEDNESDAY St. John 14:26-31

*But the Counselor, the Holy Spirit, whom the Father will
send in my name, he will teach you all things, and bring
to your remembrance all that I have said to you.* St. John
14:26

My disciples in Jerusalem could not quite believe that the
end was near. They could not understand that I would send
them another Counselor, the Holy Spirit, who would remind
them of all that I had taught them. When He comes into you,
He will bring a new Peace—like nothing you have ever experienced. He will bring a new and deeper Love and a more
abiding Joy. Confess, accept and praise!

THURSDAY St. Luke 11:13

*If you then, who are evil, know how to give good gifts to
your children, how much more will the heavenly Father
give the Holy Spirit to those who ask him!* St. Luke
11:13

My disciples, you have been doubting My Power to give
such a Gift, yet you claim to give good gifts to your children.

How much *more* will My heavenly Father give the Holy Spirit to those who ask Him, those who accept His Gift with praise and thanksgiving, those who yearn to be His temples today!

FRIDAY   St. John 7:37-39

He who believes in me, as the scripture has said, "Out of his heart shall flow rivers of living water."   St. John 7:38

Many of you have been thirsting but you knew not where to seek for the rivers of living water. Come and drink of My Spirit. If you believe in Me and claim My Spirit, you will receive these rivers of living water. My disciples had to wait until *after* I was glorified before they could receive the promised Gift. You today need only to ask, claiming this second blessing. Receive with praise to the Father.

SATURDAY   St. Luke 2:7-20

Be not afraid; for behold, I bring you good news of a great joy which will come to all the people; for to you is born this day in the city of David a Savior, who is Christ the Lord.   St. Luke 2:10 (in part)-11

My children, you have been praying for Me to incarnate Myself afresh in your hearts today. You have already cleansed the stable; you have begun to rejoice with the angels who sang of My coming, giving glory to God. With the shepherds you have come to worship Me. See Me today as the newborn baby but see also the shadow of the Cross. See Me in the Incarnation but also in the Crucifixion. See Me in the Resurrection. The same Jesus whose birth you celebrate today died and rose again to set you free! Claim Me eternally.

SUNDAY   St. Luke 1:26-38

Behold, I am the handmaid of the Lord; let it be to me according to your word.   St. Luke 1:38 (in part)

Mary heard the angel's prophecy—a greater calling than she felt capable of fulfilling, a prophecy that seemed impossible. She confirmed it with acceptance as the handmaiden of the Lord. She did not question what others might say about her: she replied, "So let it be." Will you, My child, accept whatever call comes to you in this spirit of humility and obedience? And be blessed?

MONDAY   St. Luke 1:46-55

For he who is mighty has done great things for me, and holy is his name.   St. Luke 1:49

Mary accepted the Father's call to be His instrument so that mankind would be blessed. Her praise ascended to the Father as she accepted her call to bring forth the Son through the divine empowering of the Holy Spirit. Will you be the handmaiden of the Lord: in lesser ways, His instrument of grace?

TUESDAY   St. Luke 1:67-79

And you, child, will be called the prophet of the Most High; for you will go before the Lord to prepare his ways. St. Luke 1:76

Zechariah felt the Spirit's anointing when he prophesied over his son, John. In obedience, his tongue was set free to speak words of praise to the Father. Will you let the Holy Spirit free your tongue from the shyness or pride that holds back the glorification of the Father in your life? Will you let the Holy Spirit break down any barriers so that you can praise more freely?

WEDNESDAY   Hebrews 12:1-2

Looking to Jesus the pioneer and perfecter of our faith, who for the joy that was set before him endured the cross, despising the shame, and is seated at the right hand of the throne of God.   Hebrews 12:2

The Cross in your life can be a rich gateway to My treasures if you will allow Me to do a *deep* work in your heart. You have received My baptism in the Holy Spirit but you are not allowing Me to minister freely through you. You are claiming only a superficial baptism—looking too much at signs and feelings. When you let Me do a deep cleansing of the past, more of My Power will flow through you. If enough of My children so yielded to Me, there are thousands in this city who would come out of their sin and darkness into the marvelous Light of My Kingdom—in answer to their prayers.

THURSDAY St. John 3:16; I Timothy 1:15

The saying is sure and worthy of full acceptance, that Christ Jesus came into the world to save sinners. And I am the foremost of sinners. I Timothy 1:15

Begotten of the Father's Love, I came into this world of sin so that those who would trust in Me could be saved. All had sinned and fallen short of God's purposes but My forgiveness on the Cross was mediated to *all* of mankind—all who would *receive Me* into their repentant hearts. My Blood has paid the premium for the lives of those who accept and claim this—believing, *trusting in My redemptive Love.* Like the thief on the Cross, many forfeit joyous living when they wait until their last breath to accept Me as their Savior but they will not perish, *if they believe in Me.* They, too, will experience everlasting Life—but they will have missed the comfort of My Presence in this earthly life!

FRIDAY Colossians 3:4; Revelation 21:5-8; 22:7

And behold, I am coming soon. Revelation 22:7a

Pray for My return in Power that My people may be saved. At the Second Coming, I will return to save those who have been going through the Tribulation and are yearning for My Return. You who by faith in Me have conquered in the battle of life will be My Bride, and I will give freely to you from the waters of the fountain of Life. I will be your God. I will make all things new. Behold, I am coming soon. When I appear, you will be with Me also in glory.

List of Scripture References

OLD TESTAMENT

OLD TESTAMENT

NEW TESTAMENT

NEW TESTAMENT

NEW TESTAMENT

NEW TESTAMENT

NEW TESTAMENT

NEW TESTAMENT

For more information contact:
Victorious Ministry Through Christ, Inc.
P.O. Box 1804
Winter Park, Florida 32790